CW00566646

DEDICATED TO THE MEMORY OF CHIC HENRY

To Nigel,
Not quite as good as
the cars at Goodwood
but very Australian.
Have a lovely retirement
Take care
Love Angie

LEGENDS

VOLUME THREE

PUBLISHED IN 2023 BY ARE MEDIA BOOKS, AUSTRALIA
A DIVISION OF ARE MEDIA PTY LTD

EDITOR
SIMON TELFORD

ART DIRECTOR
GAVIN MORRISON

SUB-EDITORS
BRETT COLLINGWOOD, MATT REEKIE, JENNY VALENTISH

PHOTOGRAPHY
TROY BARKER, PETER BATEMAN, DALLAS BLACKMORE, CRISTIAN BRUNELLI,
EASTON CHANG, SIMON DAVIDSON, ELLEN DEWAR, NATHAN DUFF, BRYCE FORREST, GARTSIDE, MITCH HEMMING,
BEN HOSKING, NATHAN JACOBS, GEOFF PARADISE, SHAUN TANNER, CHRIS THOROGOOD

CONTRIBUTORS
ANDREW BROADLEY, DAVE CAREY, DAVID COOK, SIMON MAJOR, GEOFF PARADISE, CRAIG PARKER, GEOFF SEDDON,
LEX SWAYN, SIMON TELFORD, GLENN TORRENS

STREET MACHINE EDITOR
ANDREW BROADLEY

OPERATIONS MANAGER – ARE MEDIA BOOKS
DAVID SCOTTO

CONTENT DIRECTOR – ENTHUSIAST
SIMON TELFORD

CHIEF REVENUE OFFICER
JOSEPH LENTHALL

CHIEF OPERATING OFFICER
SCOTT DAVISON

CHIEF EXECUTIVE OFFICER
CHRISTIAN CLARK

MAIL: UNIT 9/3-5 GILDA CT, MULGRAVE VIC 3170
EMAIL: STREETMACHINE@WHEELSMEDIA.COM.AU
WEB: STREETMACHINE.COM.AU
COPYRIGHT ARE MEDIA PTY LTD 2023
ABN 18 053 273 546
PRINTED BY LEO PAPER, CHINA
A CATALOGUE RECORD FOR THIS BOOK IS AVAILABLE FROM THE NATIONAL LIBRARY OF AUSTRALIA
ISBN-13: 978-1761221408
ORDER VIA (02) 8315 2092 (WITHIN AUSTRALIA) OR VISIT SHOP.STREETMACHINE.COM.AU

JP · 289

CONTENTS

6

FOREWORD

WELCOME to *Street Machine Legends* Volume Three! The first two volumes covered the most iconic cars to be featured in the magazine over its first 20 years and second 20 years, respectively. This time around, we're focusing on the people who've helped to make the scene what it is today.

The vast majority of those who've made it into the book started to make their impact in the 1980s or 90s. Most of them are car builders, but there are also event promoters, racers, artists, and a handful of *Street Machine* staffers. We'll cover the next 20 years' worth of legends in another format. Same goes for the real OGs from the 1960s, such as Eddie Thomas and Dale Fisher (pictured left).

Narrowing down the list to just 40 peeps was a tough job, and there were plenty of deserving folks we didn't have room for on this lap of the track. I'm talking about car builders like Ray Alldrick and Bill Jones, promoters like Ahmet 'The Mad Turk' Sehirligil, speed equipment pioneers like 'Dyno' Dave Bennett and Ron Harrop, and so many other crucial participants in our scene. We've included some cool images of a bunch of these luminaries in the next few pages as a small token of our esteem.

Putting these books together is a labour of love for the *Street Machine* team. Sifting through the archives for the best images is a blast, and we've learned some amazing things. For example, when we asked Paul Bennett to name his most important builds, he came back with a handwritten list of cars over three pages long. We knew the guy was prolific, but sheesh!

The connections between many of the people in the book are likewise fascinating. It's amazing to read about how a smartarse comment at a car show led to a young Mark Sanders helping Howard Astill on the build of ROCK 3, or the way guys like John Taverna devoted so much time to mentoring the next generation of greats.

These kinds of connections between street machine folks is all part of what makes our sport so great. The enjoyment you can have from playing with cars with your family and friends is the same, whether the build costs $5K or $5 mil.

Every small town has its own Victor Bray, its own paint and panel genius, its own tuning guru. *Street Machine*'s mission is to shine a light on as many of these figures as we can. It's a never-ending quest to unearth our sport's heroes, be they local or global, to provide recognition for them and inspiration for the rest of us. It is a task we feel privileged to pursue.

Simon Telford
EDITOR-IN-CHIEF

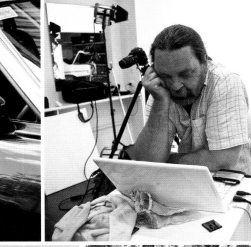

9

SUPER FLOW HEADS

After the Anglia, Milton upgraded to a
Ford Pinto that had been imported from
the US. After a two-year makeover, it ran
a best of 10.22 in SS/A. It was destroyed
in a towing accident en route to the last-
ever Surfers Paradise meeting, but was
restored by Dean Kubler in 2020

MILTON ADEY 1942-2010

TO *STREET Machine* readers of a certain age, Queenslander Milton Adey was the voice of Summernats, wielding the microphone at the event for the first 21 years of its existence.

Summernats founder, the late Chic Henry, explained to us in 2010 why he chose Milton to be his mic man: "When I started the event, I knew I had to surround myself with people who had very specific skills if I was going to pull it off.

"Milton was the obvious choice to be the burnout commentator and to work on Radio Revhead. He had such a depth of knowledge, but what really impressed me at the drags was his ability to keep the crowd entertained if we had a rain-out or some other delay — he could just continue to deliver information no matter what."

Milton's impact on the sport was not limited to the 'Nats. As a commentator, he mentored the next generation of mic jockeys, and his influence on drag racing in the 1970s and early 80s was huge, both in the commentary box and on the track as a racer and official.

"I met Milt as a newcomer to the QDRA in 1977, and he instantly made me feel welcome into the South East Queensland drag racing family," Willowbank commentator Rob Oberg told *Street Machine* in 2010. "He gave me my start in drag racing commentary soon after and helped me learn the ropes.

"In those days, supercharged cars were rare and 200mph passes even rarer. Milt told me: 'It's our job to make our sport exciting for the crowd no matter what's on track. So as long as the racing is good, commentary-wise, Stock Eliminator is as important as Top Fuel. If we get excited about it, so will the spectators.'

"Milt's dedication to drag racing stretched far beyond the commentary box. As the SQ divisional director of ANDRA he was without doubt the most effective we ever had, looking at what was best for the entire sport and not just individual interests. He had a great sense of humour and made racing fun."

STORY SIMON TELFORD **PHOTOS** MITCH HEMMING & *SM* ARCHIVES

HAWKEYE: Milton's 105E Anglia named Hawkeye ran a screaming Cosworth four-pot and held both ends of the old F/MP class record in street trim. It was later chopped and fitted with a Baker Brothers 302 and ran flat 11s like clockwork

GALAXIE: Milton's signature street car was a 429-powered sports-roof 1971 Ford Galaxie. His final build was a nostalgia-style 1928 roadster that was finished by Queensland rodder Kalvin Pollock and is now in the care of Victorian Glenn Etchell

Hawkeye

'71 Galaxie

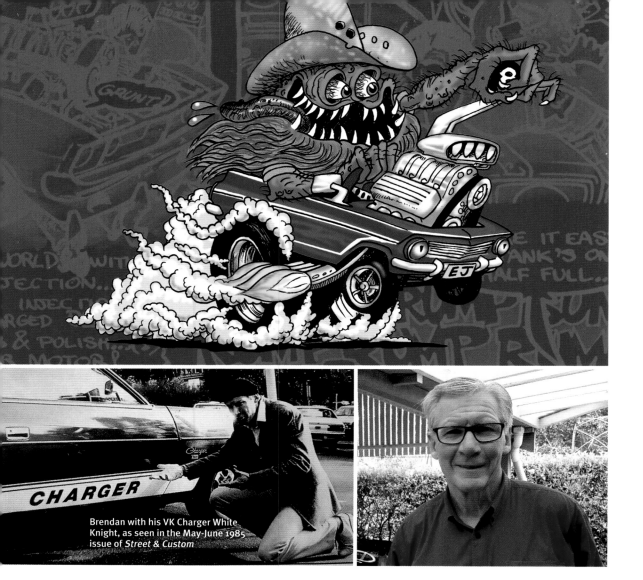

BRENDAN AKHURST 1948-2022

BRENDAN Akhurst was one of the most widely syndicated cartoonists in Australian history, but he is best known to *Street Machine* readers as the man behind the long-running *Wayne & Vicky* strip.

The adventures of Wayne Clodpole, his voluptuous girlfriend Vicky and their XP coupe were the perfect reflection of our homegrown modified car lifestyle, viewed through a screen of healthy, self-deprecating humour. The cars are beautifully drawn, instantly recognisable, but stupidly tough. You can almost feel the ground shake. And who didn't see themselves in the couple's relationship – the car-obsessed bloke and the spunky sheila who loves him anyway?

"None of us really knew where Brendan got his inspiration from, but some of the characters were based on real people," Brendan's widow Michelle says. "Wayne and Vicky were based on Brendan's neighbours when he lived in Western Sydney in the 70s. He changed Vicky's name so as not to offend."

Wayne & Vicky debuted in black and white in the Dec '81-Jan '82 issue, edited by Geoff Paradise, and went full-colour in Feb-Mar '83. The duo's last appearance first time around was in Oct-Nov '83. Perhaps BJ knew it was the last one: the strip ends with Wayne's hands turning into breasts mid-drag race and then crashing into the offices of *The Australian Women's Weekly*.

In 1984, *Wayne & Vicky* reappeared in slightly raunchier form in the Bruce Flynn and Mac Douglas-produced *Street & Custom* mag, and in *Super Street* after that.

I coaxed Brendan into bringing *Wayne & Vicky* back for another tour with *SM*, which ran from 2006 through to 2011. He also illustrated other columns, including AG Workshop, Heroic Tales and Dirty Stuff.

Wayne & Vicky was only part of a huge body of work from this prolific and talented artist over more than four decades. As well as *Maynard* in *Two Wheels* and similar cartoons for other special interest magazines, Brendan found mainstream success with syndicated newspaper comic strips *Normie* and *Louie the Fly*. He also illustrated a great many books by authors as diverse as early 20th-century poet CJ Dennis and latter-day motorcycle hard man Boris Mihailovic.

Brendan passed away in January 2022 after a short battle with cancer.

STORY GEOFF SEDDON **PHOTOS** *SM* ARCHIVES

Brendan with his VK Charger White Knight, as seen in the May-June 1985 issue of *Street & Custom*

This classic showdown between Wayne's XP and a wild A9X hatch adorned the cover of our 30th anniversary special edition

Each *Wayne & Vicky* instalment was accompanied by these two profane little gremlins named Everard and Baldwin

POR440

Mark's LS turbo-powered POR440 Val on its way to Drag Week 2017, with good mate Steve Reimann and photographer Luke Nieuwhof along for the adventure

MARK ARBLASTER

KNOWN to all as 'Arby', Mark Arblaster joined the *Street Machine* team in the April 2000 issue and has been penning his Urban Warfare column for the magazine ever since.

"Not only does he write in an entertaining manner, he backs up his opinions with hard-earned street cred," wrote then-editor Geoff Seddon of that first appearance.

Seddo credits Arby with helping him settle into the editor's chair while embodying the outlaw spirit Seddo was striving to capture in the mag: "I'd been in the job about two minutes when Arby picked me up in WAR440 and took me up to Newcastle for a burnout comp. I thought, 'Wow! This guy has balls!'"

Seddo teamed Mark up with some of Australia's best photographers for a series of gonzo-style stories on events that had never been covered by the mag before, including illegal street racing, private burnout comps and plenty of cruising in questionably legal street cars.

Mark made his name with his white and purple-striped WAR440 VG Valiant, competing with vigour on the burnout pad, dyno and drag strip. After trying his hand at promoting with his series of Revfest events, Arby became enamoured with *Hot Rod* Drag Week and has competed in that event multiple times in various cars.

A new version of WAR440 was constructed in 2011. This time the car had enough show to take out multiple awards at Meguiar's MotorEx, but it was designed specifically to take on drag and drive-style events, with a ProCharged, 500-cube big-block mill up front.

While a planned Drag Week trip fell through, the car successfully competed in the first *Street Machine* Drag Challenge, where it took out first place in the Outlaw Blown class and won Quickest Mopar.

For his next trick, Arby bolted together POR440, a turbo LS-powered VG coupe that he shipped over and drove across the US for the start of Drag Week 2017, before successfully completing the event with a best of 9.441 seconds.

Arby's most recent drag-and-drive adventure was a gremlin-plagued attack on the 2022 Rocky Mountain Race Week 2.0 in a blown Chevy Malibu.

Since then, he's been busy throwing birthday parties for both WAR440 and POR440.

STORY SIMON TELFORD **PHOTOS** *SM* ARCHIVES

ABOVE: The reborn WAR440 took on the very first *Street Machine* Drag Challenge in 2014, winning trophies for first in Outlaw Blown and Quickest Mopar

BELOW: In its original guise, WAR440 went through countless engine configurations, including nitrous-fed, blown and injected, and ProCharged

HOWARD ASTILL

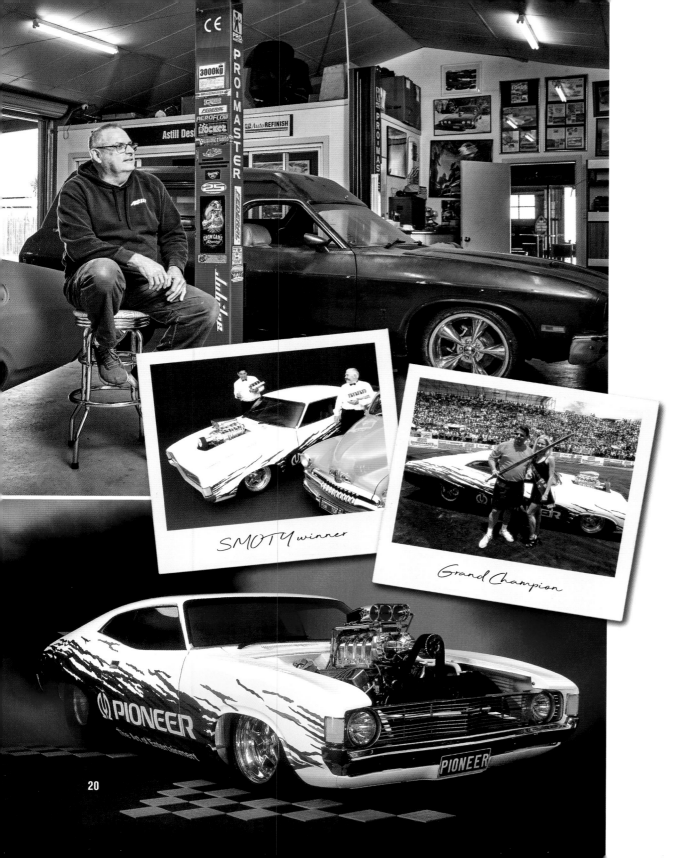

SMOTY winner

Grand Champion

PIONEER
The Art of Entertainment

PIONEER

THE BLOKE FROM BROKEN HILL

HOWARD Astill is, without question, one of the all-time greats of Aussie street machining. Howard has spent decades on the tools building countless top-shelf show cars both for himself and for customers. He has won just about everything there is to win, including Street Machine of the Year in 1995, and *Street Machine* Summernats Grand Champion in 1991, 1992 and 1997. He's also won the Master Craftsman award and is a Rare Spares Legend, so he's about as highly decorated as they come.

Howard got his start in the sport in his hometown of Broken Hill in the late 70s, and he's still hard at work as a one-man band in his Astill Designs home workshop, churning out high-end builds for customers at an impressive rate of knots.

"I've been at it a long time!" says Howard. "I started back in the late 70s. My cousins and brother all had different types of cars and I got into panel vanning. Then when we had a baby, I went to a four-door with my ROCK SOLID XA, went to the '86 and '88 Nationals and had a fair bit of success at those, then I rebuilt that car into ROCK 3, which is the blue Falcon most people know.

"I went on a roll from there and built a '63 Fairlane for *Street Machine*; the Pioneer coupe, which was 1994 to '96; then a '66 Mustang that debuted at Summernats 21."

Since then, he's been building cars for customers. Peter Lewis's XC that debuted at Summernats 35 is number 15 of the Astill Design cars.

PREVIOUS PAGES (18-19): ROCK 4 was a Compact Fairlane Howard built for *Street Machine* as a giveaway car. Howard bought the car back for Summernats 17, driving it to Canberra from Broken Hill, where it scored another Top 60 berth. It later copped a rebuild by Peter Fitzpatrick for then-owner Gary Reid

LEFT: The trophy-winning Pioneer XA Falcon coupe. It shared the 1995 Street Machine of the Year spoils with Darryl McBeth and his FJ Holden.

Howard would then go on to collect his third Grand Champion win at Summernats 1997

RIGHT: This is how we rolled in the late 1980s. Despite being one of the winningest show cars of its time, the transition from ROCK 2 to ROCK 3 was still done in Howard's shed with fairly basic gear

TOP RIGHT: Howard and wife Heather at the Riverland Cruise in 1990, with son Lee and Tony Baohm of twin-Predator 1971 Trans Am fame

Riverland Cruise

Van Nationals

ABOVE: Howard with his wife Heather and their XC van at the 1978 Van Nationals at Halls Gap. "In those days, you could cruise along at 180km/h in the country and it was just normal behaviour!" says Howard

LEFT: At the time of writing, Howard's latest completed project was Peter Lewis's incredible XC Falcon, which combines an FG Falcon dash and underpinnings with an 8.6L

Jon Kaase Boss Nine motor and stunning detail

RIGHT: Howard had some new tricks for ROCK SOLID 2, like dumping the springs for coil-overs and fitting an hydraulic handbrake

BOTTOM RIGHT: Adam and Kylie Perry's Tailspin FB Holden is one of 15 cars Howard has built or collaborated on under the Astill Design banner

"Astill Design is pretty much boutique," says Howard. "I like to work with a customer who's got a story. Adam and Kylie Perry's Tailspin FB Holden is a great example. They approached me on advice from a friend of theirs, and that has become a lifelong friendship. What I loved about that project and why I put a lot of extra time into it was their eagerness to learn and grow and develop with the car.

"What they asked me when they first came to me was whether I would teach them to build a car. I spoke to the wife about it and I felt that at my age that's something I should be doing; to try and pass it on. Adam and Kylie have taken it on gangbusters and will go on to build a lot of cars, which makes that story nice. Having a big-dollar customer doesn't necessarily interest me; it's more about helping someone achieve their goals, keeping my hand in what I love, and paying a few bills.

"I do have a car of my own on the go. It's an XC panel van, so I'm going back to my roots, I guess. We've managed to pick up a four-speed, BorgWarner, air con, power steer, Rally Pack car from an auction. I'm now in the process of rebuilding that, and it'll be more old-school with a bit of current flavour in that it'll have 18-inch wheels and a bit bigger brakes. I'm sticking with the single-rail gearbox and the BorgWarner rear, but everything will be done nicely."

STORY ANDREW BROADLEY **PHOTOS** *SM* ARCHIVES

Tailspin

ABOVE: Ron accepting the tinware from *Street Machine* editor Tim Britten at Summernats 3 in 1990

RIGHT: Peter Bateman's iconic shot of Ron's ute for the Jan-Feb 1991 cover remains one of the most memorable in the history of *Street Machine*

RON BARCLAY

IT'S hard to think of a more influential Aussie street machine than Ron Barclay's HQ Holden ute. We'll never know how many folks were inspired by Ron's less-is-more approach to building cars, but the numbers must be huge.

The ute's popularity with the general public was proven by it winning both People's Choice at Summernats and the Street Machine of the Year award in 1990. This was no mean feat, since it was up against the likes of Howard Astill's Rock 3, Rob Beauchamp's Calais and Alan Fleming's HG panel van – all very popular cars both then and now.

The ute also excelled at the highest levels of judging, winning Top Judged at the 'Nats in both 1990 and 1995.

The HQ's design and execution was very different to most of the competition. Rather than throwing wild mods and stacks of go-fast gear at his hay hauler, Ron focused his attention on the details.

"Back then, I was reading the US mags and watching what guys like Boyd Coddington were doing, so I built the ute like a Coddington car," Ron says. "But I went a bit different with the colour; the Yanks weren't even using pastels back then. My mates gave me hell over the coral colour, but then I cleaned up at Canberra and all of a sudden they didn't think it was so bad after all."

Show judges loved the ute because it steered away from chrome and braid, and the readers loved that it was built on a budget. The best way to describe Ron's ute is 'minimalist'. The chassis, engine, gearbox and diff were all so clean that you'd let your toddlers play with them.

After selling the ute in 1996, Ron bought it back in 2011. "If you look at show cars now, the ute isn't that far off the mark," he reckons. "The only thing I don't like about the car now is the brushed aluminium."

Eventually, Ron plans to rebuild the Quey, but he's got to finish his track-inspired '67 Camaro first. He also built a slick '32 Ford coupe, which we featured back in March 2005.

STORY SIMON TELFORD **PHOTOS** CHRIS THOROGOOD & *SM* ARCHIVES

VL makeover

'67 Nova

Rob upped the ante with regard to the competition elements for his VL Calais pro streeter, with a full competition interior and extensive rollcage nestled within the confines of the Holden bodyshell

ROB BEAUCHAMP

WHEN Rob Beauchamp debuted his revamped LX Torana at the 1986 Street Machine Nationals, he turned the hot car scene on its ear. Sure, he'd made waves with the carbied version of the car at the same event in 1984, but this makeover was next level. It featured the pedantic attention to detail that would become Rob's calling card, with sharp panel and paintwork, a trimmed interior, polished aluminium, and an injected 350 Chevy powering it to the business end of pro street.

The LX became an instant legend, but Rob wasn't one to rest on his laurels. The dust had barely settled on his tinware raid on the '86 Nationals when he sold the Torana as a roller and prepared to launch his next attack on the pro street genre – his legendary VL Calais.

Rob was keen for a late-model pro streeter and liked the slipperier shape that the then-current VL Calais had to offer. The basic shell was outfitted with a tubular chassis and Funny Car-style rollcage by Bill Jones at Weldwell Engineering, before an Enderle-injected 302-cube Chev was detailed to the max and slotted in. Metallic grey paint and polished Center Line Auto Drags sorted the exterior.

A makeover in grape purple and Weld Pro Star wheels followed. Both guises combined to score Rob and the Calais three Grand Champion titles at the first three Summernats, blowing minds but also igniting fierce debate about the place of pro street cars in the scene.

A near two-decade hiatus from car builds followed, but Rob burst back into the spotlight with his stunning '67 Chevy Nova (*SM*, Aug '11), complete with a mix of CV8 Monaro and V-series Commodore LS1 underpinnings. The more street-oriented focus of this build was obvious, but it still featured Rob's show-level attention to detail and engineering perfection.

Rob and his wife Jan enjoyed the fruits of their labour before selling the Nova in 2017, replacing the compact with a second-gen Camaro. Although adamant that the Camaro would remain generally as-bought, old habits die hard, and the car has since been subjected to the Beauchamp touch.

STORY SIMON MAJOR **PHOTOS** *SM* ARCHIVES

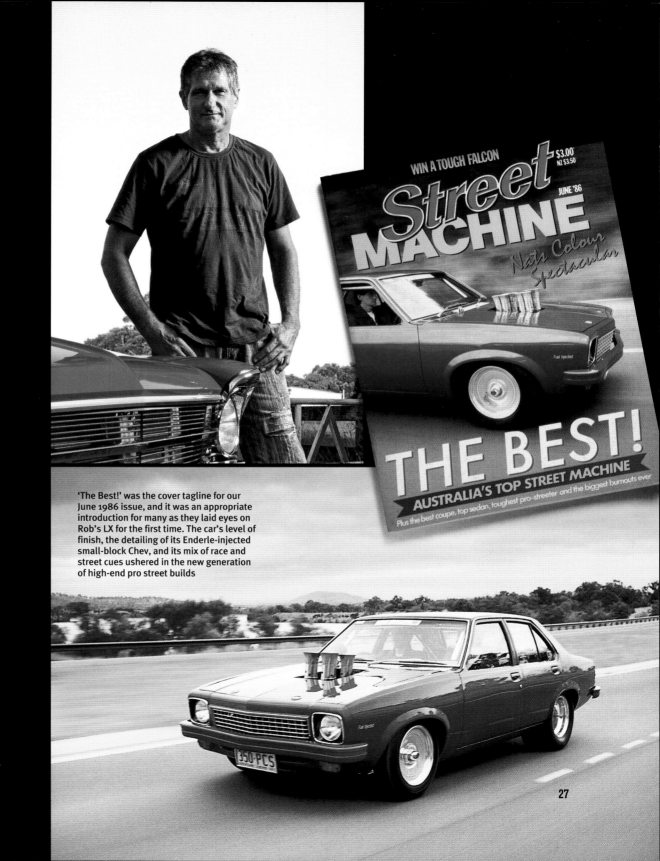

'The Best!' was the cover tagline for our June 1986 issue, and it was an appropriate introduction for many as they laid eyes on Rob's LX for the first time. The car's level of finish, the detailing of its Enderle-injected small-block Chev, and its mix of race and street cues ushered in the new generation of high-end pro street builds

FC wagon

'36 Chevy transporter

ABOVE: Two of our fave Beach-built feature cars were Mitch Reinders's tough FC Holden wagon (*SM*, Dec '09) and the same guy's incredible chopped '36 Chev transporter (*SM*, Mar '11)

GREG 'BEACH' BALL

IF THE spirit of the early Summernats could be encapsulated in one image, it may be that of a grinning Greg 'Beach' Ball, iconic tit hat on his head, cruising around in a lidless Valiant called NATEX.

A panel beater and spray painter by trade, Greg cut his post-apprenticeship teeth building hot rods and Lincolns for Kevin Monk. He then worked for a mob doing soft-top conversions on Valiant hardtops. He estimates he did around 180 of 'em, including a couple for himself that brought him some notoriety on the booming street machine scene.

"My white Valiant (*SM*, Apr-May '88) won Top Convertible at Summernats 1, which was a real highlight for me," says Greg. "But most people know me for the pink one I built after that (*SM*, Apr-May '89). The pink one was way more fun, because with the white one we spent all our time cleaning and polishing it for the show 'n' shine. We just sank piss and cruised the pink one for four days."

Greg sold the pink Val soon after starting up Pro Street Restorations on Sydney's Northern Beaches in 1989. We documented the wild scene that sprang up around that little shop in the Oct-Nov '91 issue.

After 21 years at the one address, Greg moved Pro Street Restorations to the Hunter Valley to much bigger premises and a change of pace. Current customer projects include an insane but fully engineered XA coupe with Kaase Boss Nine power, a Hellcat-powered VH Charger, and a wild Albion COE truck.

Greg's dream build is an XP Falcon coupe that he's had on the go since 1980. It was his first car.

"It's been through four colour changes, numerous engine combos and I still haven't driven it!" he says. "Now it is a full-chassis deal, tubbed with big 'n' little Convos, with a 12-inch engine set-back and unmuffled zoomies! Because of the chassis mods, it would need to be registered as an ICV here, but there is no way I can bring it up to 2023 ADRs, so it will go to the US, where I can take it on Power Tour and drive the wheels off it."

STORY CRAIG PARKER **PHOTOS** PETER BATEMAN

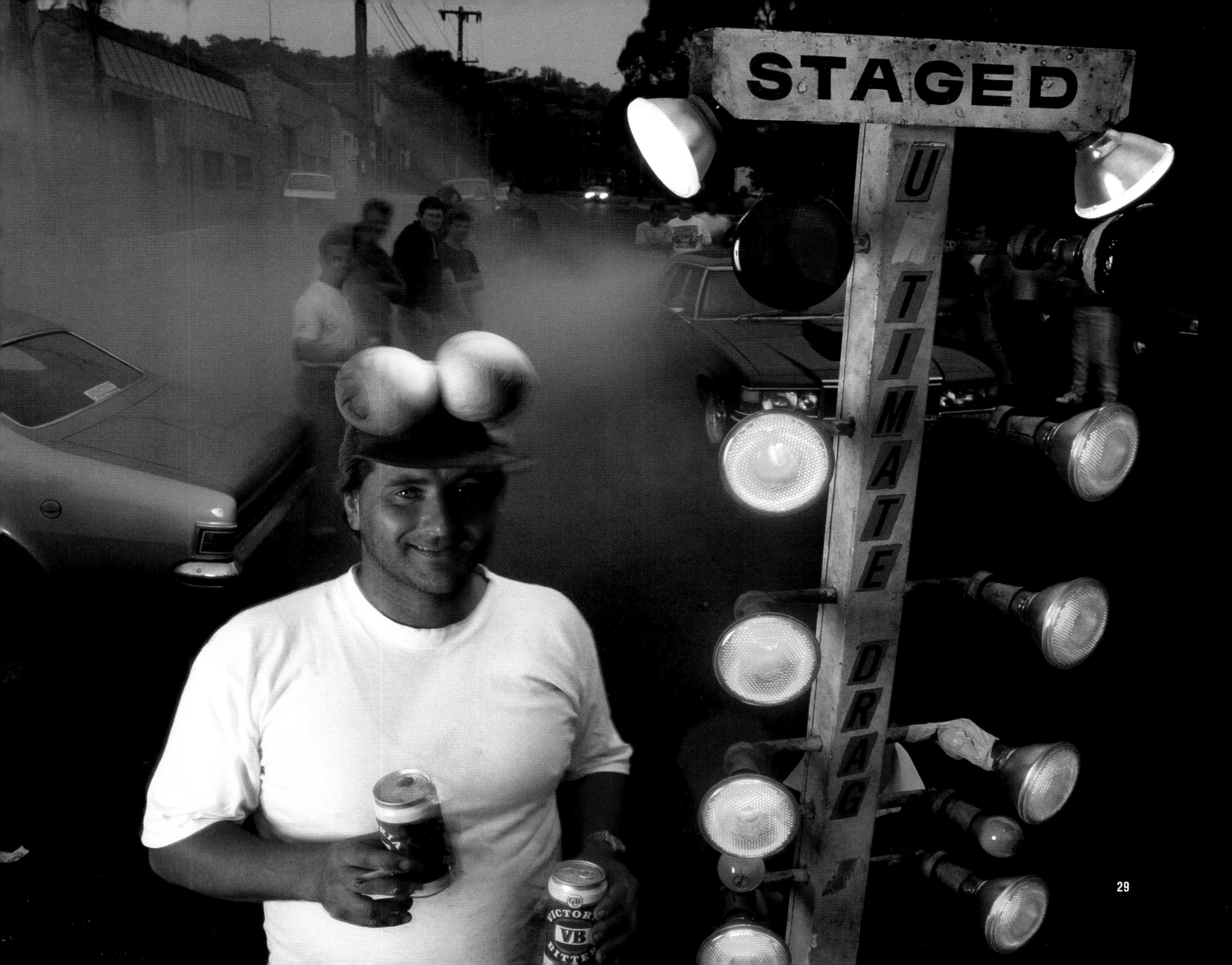
STAGED
VB

Road testing and tuning the Castrol
Coupe at Oran Park for the September
1986 issue of *Street Machine*

KEVIN BARTLETT

KEVIN Bartlett is one of Australia's most decorated race drivers. He's a Bathurst champion, two-time Gold Star recipient, Macau Grand Prix winner and has piloted everything from Indy Cars to Paul Halstead's diabolical De Tomaso Pantera.

In addition to that, KB was *Street Machine*'s technical editor for almost 30 years – from June '86 to December 2014 – answering questions in his KB's Workshop column, penning tech yarns, and building some of our most famous project cars.

KB was brought on by then-editor Phil Scott as part of the latter's plan to professionalise and supercharge the magazine.

KB's answers to the questions that flowed in each month ran the gamut, from in-depth replies through to pithy expressions of exasperation. For example, when asked in the September '86 issue how much it would cost to drop a Ford 250 six into an HG Holden to replace a sad 186, KB bluntly told the guy to either buy a Ford or reco the red motor! On the same page, he went into detail explaining to an RX-3 owner how to correctly jet his Holley. In short, the quality of the answer was directly proportional to the quality of the question.

Projects overseen by KB included the first of Phil Scott's big-buck giveaway cars, the evergreen HQFORU Monaro. That was followed by the Castrol Coupe XB Falcon, the Castrol A9X, the ONE HO TO GO XF Falcon and a targa-top Corvette, amongst others.

Kev also had a long working relationship with Kerry Packer – the guy who owned *Street Machine* for many years as part of his Australian Consolidated Press empire. Kerry funded KB's ambitious Group C Camaro team via a Channel 9 sponsorship, and KB was Kerry's go-to guy for his personal hot car addiction. This included overseeing the development of twin turbos on Packer's XJ-S Jag so it could keep pace with the Porsche of radio titan John Laws.

Legend has it that on one occasion Packer broke down in the car on the way to Canberra and flew Bartlett in via helicopter to fix the problem. The chopper landed on Lake George, Kerry jumped in it and left KB to it!

STORY SIMON TELFORD **PHOTOS** *SM* ARCHIVES

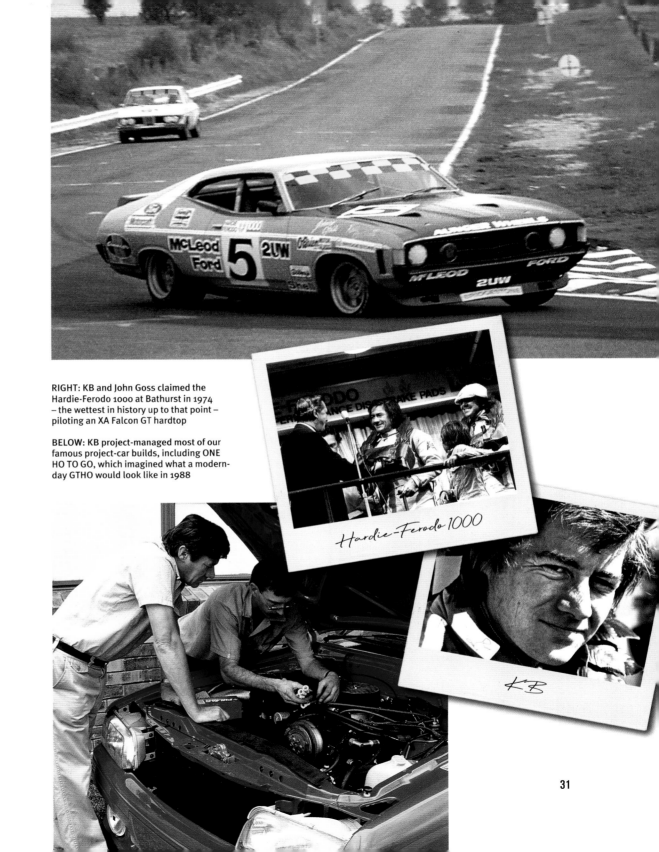

RIGHT: KB and John Goss claimed the Hardie-Ferodo 1000 at Bathurst in 1974 – the wettest in history up to that point – piloting an XA Falcon GT hardtop

BELOW: KB project-managed most of our famous project-car builds, including ONE HO TO GO, which imagined what a modern-day GTHO would look like in 1988

LEFT: LITRE8 was engineered from the ground up to be driven in anger at the track. The 343mm front rotors and four-pot AP Racing calipers were enormous for their day, while Bilstein shocks, optimised suspension geometry, a braced and stitch-welded chassis, and 17x10in Compomotive wheels wearing 265in-wide Dunlop slicks mean there's so much more to this amazing car than just its awesome driveline

BELOW: Howard is a software engineer by trade, but he's pretty handy on the spanners and has always tackled a good amount of the mechanical work on LITRE8 himself. Nankervis Performance Boats did the engine rebuild, but Howard immensely enjoyed the process of tinkering in the shed, fitting the car back up

HOWARD BELL

HOWARD Bell's relationship with his iconic LX SL/R 5000 Torana, known as LITRE8, has spanned four decades and counting. He bought it brand new in April 1976 for $6800 – his annual salary at the time – and managed to leave it stock for three months.

"It just evolved over the years," says Howard. "Once you get the sniff, you always need more."

After Howard played around with the stock 308 for a while, a mechanic mate suggested switching to a six with the top-of-the-line Normalair-Garrett Strata 6 kit. The Torana then spent the next 10 years powered by various turbo sixes, but, according to Howard, "it was always on that fine line: a winner or a grenade."

A new era began when a mate offered to buy the engine, and Howard ended up with an alloy Keith Black LS7. "It ran a MoTeC ECU and a Kinsler intake that had been designed to fit under the bonnet of a Corvette and set me back $5000!" Howard says. "A second rebuild in 2000 saw me go to Edelbrock heads. That lasted until a track day in January 2017. It went like a scalded cat, but that was its swan song."

For its latest refresh, Howard retained the KB alloy block and Kinsler intake but added new heads and internals. "All that added up to 564 cubes and likely low-to-mid 900s in terms of horsepower," he says. "It will no longer be LITRE8 in its capacity [now 9.243 litres], but the LITRE8 plates and SL/R 8000 stencils will remain, true to the car's 28-year origins as a KB 479ci BBC."

While the pro touring genre never took off in Australia like it did in the US, LITRE8 and a handful of other cars like Craig Parker's TUFFXY were pro tourers before the term was even invented.

"Pro street was king back then," recalls Howard. "There were incredible cars like Rick Dobbertin's Pontiac J2000 and Rob Beauchamp's Torana. I never really coined a term for what my car was, but I think of it as a pro circuit car."

STORY ANDREW BROADLEY
PHOTOS NATHAN JACOBS, SHAUN TANNER & *SM* ARCHIVES

MotorEx 2012

Paul's utterly insane Borgward Goliath
was built to take on Targa-style events,
but it was so sharp and innovative that
it won Best of Breed Street Machine at
MotorEx 2012

Paul's '69 Camaro

PAUL BENNETT

CANADIAN-born, Blue Mountains-based car builder Paul Bennett has had a hand in creating a raft of seriously iconic cars. We could fill a book with cars that feature his handiwork, but just to paint a quick picture of his contributions down the decades, his résumé includes George Anthony's pro street XB sedan in the 80s, Darryl McBeth's Xplod Commodore delivery in the 90s, Anthony Sant's '57 in the 00s, and Nathan Borg's Grand Champion-winning Datsun ute in the 10s. Not to mention Paul's own builds, which are rolling manifestations of his fertile imagination and fierce individuality.

Paul got his start working in Alberta in the 1970s oil boom and found a steady stream of cashed-up customers. While there, he built his first car, a rusty '69 Camaro that he turned into an early pro streeter, which scored big on the International Show Car Association circuit.

In search of better weather and a more relaxed lifestyle, Paul moved to Australia in the early 80s and became a sought-after car builder, with a flair for airbrushing and graphics. The latter was captured in all its glory on the cover of the September 1995 issue of *Street Machine*, which featured Paul's pink '68 Camaro (his first build for himself after arriving Down Under) and Brian Horsman's yellow '68 Corvette. Both cars were cutting-edge for the time, and they remain instantly recognisable as Bennett designs.

Paul didn't build another car for himself until his '42 Willys (*SM*, Apr '07). This car featured Indigenous Dreamtime-themed graphics, a wild all-steel custom dash, pro touring-spec underpinnings, and quad-cam Mustang V8 mechanicals.

Mick Barbero's Gemini

Wayne Jeffress's HR

The Willys build was dedicated to Paul's late father. "I had the car well underway in paint and had laid out much of the artwork when I lost my dad," he says. "The Aboriginal Dreamtime theme was something that I'd wanted to do for years but I never found a customer with the guts. This was the perfect opportunity. I had Dad's words in the back of my head: 'Always do exactly what you want to do. Do things as you please.'"

While the Willys was both innovative and individual, Paul's crowning achievement in both of those departments was his mind-bending Borgward Goliath (*SM*, Nov '12). Paul recreated the Goliath – and matching trailer – as a surf wagon-themed concept that could double as a long-distance touring car and a track day warrior. Every aspect of the car was modified beyond recognition, and, while it was schmick enough to win Best of Breed Street Machine at MotorEx 2012, it was also utterly practical and useable.

Aside from his long list of completed cars, Paul has a number of builds that were done to a point, handed back to the owners, and are yet to see the light of day, including a high-end pro touring HQ Monaro owned by Silvio Muscat and a heavily modified '67 Mustang fastback belonging to Nick Pedotis. Paul reckons both cars are show-stoppers and he'd love to see them finished.

Paul has recently put his car collection – and the wild residence he built to house them – up for sale so he can see out his days pursuing his other great passion of travel.

TOP LEFT: Paul's '68 Camaro SS (*SM*, Sep '95) featured his signature graphics, this time with a North American Indian theme. Bodywork was extensive, with a raised flat floor, fabbed firewall and late-model dash

MIDDLE LEFT: The Xplod Commodore sedan delivery was Darryl McBeth's follow-up to his SMOTY-winning FJ. *Street Machine* followed the build of the car in detail, including Paul's work on the body, chassis and paint

BOTTOM LEFT: Anthony Sant's '57 (*SM*, Feb '04) remains a landmark Aussie build. Paul handled the chassis and rear suspension build, and the epic bodywork

STORY SIMON TELFORD **PHOTOS** PETER BATEMAN & *SM* ARCHIVES

George Anthony's XB

Peter Jackson's taxi-themed, rotary-powered Austin A30 (*SM*, May '03) is another Bennett build pushing into the realms of concept car. It landed in the Top 10 and won PPG Supreme at Summernats 16

Peter Jackson's Austin A30

Nathan Borg's Datsun ute

Paul originally built his Willys as a pro streeter on a chrome-moly chassis, but pivoted to pro touring with a Mustang mod motor for power, a wild mirror-image steel dash, and radical underpinnings including massive Alcon brakes

SUPERFORMANCE
· V-8 ENGINES · (07) 202 4400 · SPEED EQUIPMENT·

ENTRANT

Chevrolet

QUEENSLAND · SUNSHINE STATE

Castrol

Summernats

A chance meeting with burnout pioneer
John Peterson wised Victor up on just
how much fun a real burnout could be.
Appearances at the Street Machine
Nationals and early Summernats in the
four-door, as well as a feature in the
June '87 issue of *Street Machine*, marked
the beginnings of a national profile

VICTOR BRAY

OF ALL the legends in this book, Queensland drag racer Victor Bray would perhaps be the most recognisable to your average Australian. The idea of a genial, Bundy rum-sipping tomato farmer piloting an insane black '57 Chev to six ANDRA Top Doorslammer Championships on the trot is fairly memorable.

Victor combined that success with great marketing nous, trademark burnouts and a Brock-like common touch to build a massive, loyal following. A *Street Machine* column that ran from 1993 until 2021 didn't hurt, either.

Victor's racing career began on the street and took off in earnest when he slotted a 307 Chev into his undercoat-covered four-door '57. He then discovered the addictive qualities of nitrous oxide thanks to local giggle-gas pioneer Bob Hamilton. Victor paid for countless bottles of the stuff with loads of veggies left on Bob's doorstep, and the tatty-looking '57 took plenty of money from unsuspecting Flash Harrys all the way from Brisbane to Bundaberg.

Victor tried drag racing for real at Surfers Paradise Raceway and was soon hooked. He gained a mentor in the form of the late Mick Atholwood, who guided him away from nitrous and into the welcoming arms of a blown, injected small-block. Victor quickly became a force to be reckoned with at the early Wild Bunch meets for blown cars in the late 80s at Willowbank Raceway.

The alcohol donk aside, the four-door '57 was getting too quick for its own good, and in the early 90s Victor graduated to his first real race car, albeit one built on a budget with a One Tonner chassis, but with Keith Black power.

Proper Murray Anderson-built race cars followed, and, thus equipped, Victor won six Top Doorslammer Championships between 1996 and 2001, and set numerous Australian and world records.

He also watched proudly as son Ben won two Top Doorslammer Championships and a Top Alcohol Championship of his own. Ben also branched out into Sport Compact racing with much success.

A serious skin cancer scare put a pause on Victor's racing in 2017, but he returned to a rapturous reception at the 2018 Winternationals.

STORY SIMON TELFORD **PHOTOS** *SM* ARCHIVES

BOTTOM RIGHT: The Wild Bunch graduated to full-fledged Group One status for the 1995-'96 season, and a number of tours by American racers, including Kirk Kuhns, Jim Campos (those two seen here hamming it up with Victor for *Street Machine*), John Scialpi, Scotty Cannon and Johnny Rocca, helped propel the class to mass popularity

BELOW: Ben and Victor lifted Team Bray's profile to a whole new level by running their burnout cars at 'straight' motorsport events, including the Australian F1 Grand Prix, the Gold Coast IndyCar meets and V8 Supercars rounds. Victor once did a tyre-frying lap of Mount Panorama that took 14 minutes and used 235 litres of methanol!

Victor and Mick Atholwood, '91

Wild Bunch era

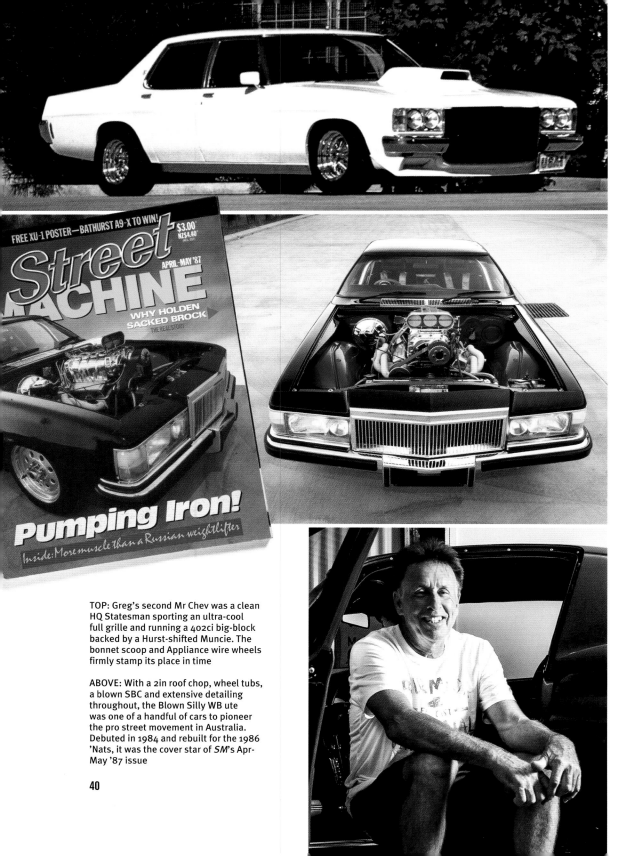

GREG CARLSON

THE name Greg Carlson is synonymous with pioneering 1980s street machine builds. As part of the Queensland-based Beauchamp/Carlson/Pagel trio that set the hot-car scene alight, Greg and his pro street Holdens played a major role in shaping the street machining hobby in this country.

He's best remembered for his Blown Silly pairing – the chopped, blown black WB ute and jaw-dropping silver pro street VK Calais. These cars combined show car detailing with drag strip performance. "I think one of the reasons I won so many trophies is my obsession with the smallest details," says Greg. "I'd spend countless hours refining everything until it was just perfect in my eyes."

His first full-on build was an EH van powered by a 327 Chev that he sold to finish an HQ van called Mr Chev, which featured a brand-spanking WB Statesman front and ran a small-block Chev and Muncie combo. "I eventually stepped away from vans as the street machine scene came into its own," says Greg. He then built a second Mr Chev based on an HQ Statesman that featured a full-grille HZ front along with a 402 big-block and four-speed.

Greg's black WB ute was a brand-new bodyshell that was given a two-inch roof chop and a set of wheel tubs. In its first incarnation, it ran a carb-fed blown 350 Chev, with Dragways and a WB Statesman front. The ute scored Best Engineered when it debuted at the 1984 Street Machine Nationals in Canberra. It was rebuilt for the '86 Nationals with a heap more detailing, Weld wheels and injection, earning Best Engineered again, plus Top Undercarriage/Driveline.

The VK Calais, however, is the most famous of Greg's builds. From its blown and injected small-block Chev to its polished alloy interior, it featured state-of-the-art race engineering and incredible attention to detail. Greg came up trumps at the first Summernats in 1988 with awards for Best Engineered, Top Street Competition and Entrants' Choice.

In more recent times, Greg has gravitated towards American cars, with a '68 Camaro and '67 Corvette sharing shed space with his early builds. "I just love clean, tough cars, and that is what I've always strived to build," he says.

STORY SIMON MAJOR **PHOTOS** *SM* ARCHIVES

TOP: Greg's second Mr Chev was a clean HQ Statesman sporting an ultra-cool full grille and running a 402ci big-block backed by a Hurst-shifted Muncie. The bonnet scoop and Appliance wire wheels firmly stamp its place in time

ABOVE: With a 2in roof chop, wheel tubs, a blown SBC and extensive detailing throughout, the Blown Silly WB ute was one of a handful of cars to pioneer the pro street movement in Australia. Debuted in 1984 and rebuilt for the 1986 'Nats, it was the cover star of *SM*'s Apr-May '87 issue

Greg's VK build was supremely cutting-edge for 1988. It featured a blown-and-injected small-block, a full aluminium interior, two motorbike calipers on each wheel, and the rear axles were so short they would fit in a shoebox!

RIGHT: Mario's son Andy, his wife Catriona and Mario with WILD CAD at the 2012 West Coast Kustoms Cruisin' Nationals in California, where the Caddy placed in the Top Five Wild Kustoms

California 2012

42

MARIO COLALILLO 1958-2018

MORE than a few folks in this book are famous simply for building one iconic car. A smaller number kicked on to create an entire body of work. Mario Colalillo was one of the latter.

Like many young blokes growing up in Western Sydney in the 1970s, Mario was into hot Holdens and racing at Brickies. But he was always reading *Custom Rodder* and knew the older stuff was where it was at.

The first car he bought was a '39 Plymouth coupe. "I've had the Plymouth since I was 17," Mario told *SM* in 2009. "I saw it sitting under a willow tree and hounded the bloke for six months. It was an old custom built by a guy called George Clark in the 60s."

Mario turned it into a jet-black street rod with a tough small-block and Muncie combo that was good enough to score a feature in *Australian Street Rodding*. It was to be the first of many magazine features Mario would receive over the next 30-plus years.

More rods followed, including a trad '34 roadster, a bad-arse '34 coupe, and a flamed '40 pick-up, all of which oozed style in spades.

Early in the new millennium, the '39 copped a pro street revamp, with tubs, a ground-scraping stance, and a high-revving blown and injected small-block that sucked meth and powered the car to nine-second quarters. It was so cool that we featured it in the August 2002 issue.

Everything changed when Mario bought a cheap '63 Pontiac Parisienne and turned into a spectacular chopped cruiser for under 10 grand. He was hooked, and henceforth dedicated himself to preaching the gospel of the custom.

Following his epiphany came a pair of widely ambitious Caddys, the first a '55 Coupe DeVille dubbed KING CAD, which featured a four-inch chop, deleted quarter-vent windows, a '59 Chev dash, wild blue metal-flake paint, and leather tuck-and-roll trim. Matched to a slammed stance, the '55 was the first of its kind to ever grace the cover of *Street Machine* (Sep '03).

Next was a '59 dubbed WILD CAD. This car featured insane custom bodywork inside and out, and a fade-job by US custom godfather Gene Winfield. It scored Mario another *SM* cover in October 2010.

'34 roadster

ABOVE: The chopped 1963 Pontiac Parisienne was a fun cruiser project built for under $10K in the early 2000s. It was Mario's first experiment with building a custom, and he was immediately hooked

LEFT: The '55 DeVille dubbed KING CAD featured a host of custom work, including a 4in chop that removed the quarter-vent windows

BELOW: Mario built this way-cool FB Holden van from a stuffed FB ute, complete with a Gene Winfield chop and fade-job

After debuting WILD CAD at MotorEx in 2010, the car was shipped to the US to tackle the show scene for 12 months, starting with the invite-only Long Beach Motorama. But following the car's appearance at SEMA in Las Vegas, Mario's body told him it was time to slow down. The stress and physical effort he'd poured into getting the '59 on display resulted in Mario taking a turn that led to quadruple-bypass surgery and a premature trip back home.

Mario's son Andy was tasked with escorting the Caddy through the rest of its tour, including a triumphant appearance at the 2011 Grand National Roadster Show, where it scored the Barris Kustom D'Elegance Award – presented by George Barris himself – and Top Radical Custom Hardtop. This was followed by the Sacramento Autorama, where Mario won the prized King of Kustom ring, joining the likes of John D'Agostino and James Hetfield.

Mario loved that ring, but the Barris award was the one he prized the most. "To be chosen by a guy like that in that kind of company is about as good as it gets to me," he told us in a 2011 interview.

Mario soon recovered and kept creating rolling artwork, including a chopped FB Holden van that was built, in part, to encourage the younger crew to get out there and utilise our native raw material.

Doggedly determined to increase the profile and popularity of customs in Australia, Mario's relationship with Gene Winfield saw him bring the master craftsman Down Under to paint cars, hold metalworking courses and energise the next generation of custom fiends.

Mario also orchestrated the Kavalcade of Kustoms at MotorEx 2012, a show within a show that featured a curated display of custom cars that has yet to be matched locally. The event is still spoken about in reverent tones, and you can bet more than a few builds were inspired by the group of cars Mario brought together.

Mario passed away from a heart attack on 12 November 2018 at the age of 60. Far too early for his family and many friends, and far too early for a guy who still had plenty of cars to build and fish to catch.

STORY BORIS VISKOVIC **PHOTOS** PETER BATEMAN & *SM* ARCHIVES

'40 Ford pick-up

'39 Plymouth coupe

AA/HR
2980

VP Racing Synthetic Oil

Terry's Diff & Chassis   EAGLE MOTORSPORT   John Kuiper Autos

Mario was one of the original Australian Nostalgia Racers and developed his '39 Plymouth into an absolute weapon of a street rod, running a best ET of 9.03. His son Andy has plans to bring it back as a bad-arse street car

45

Psycho III was the beginning of big things for Graeme and Wendy, running a wheel-spinning best of 7.53@207mph. The car was sold to fund the couple's first business, but they've since built a tribute car that competes alongside their Outlaw Nitro Funny Cars

Psycho III

Graeme and Wendy

GRAEME COWIN

GRAEME Cowin and his wife Wendy are legends of the Australian drag racing scene, as record-setting racers, team owners, series sponsors, event promoters, and as the owners of both Rocket Industries and Aeroflow Performance.

Graeme's path to drag racing began when he worked around the startline at Castlereagh in the mid 60s. A few squirts in his street Customline convinced him to convert a hot rod he was building into a race car by fitting a Fiat Topolino body and leaving off the fruit.

Graeme was hooked, and he then built the blown small-block Chev-powered Psycho II, with Wendy Johns (before they were married) as co-owner. In 1970, it became the first Aussie altered to run a nine-second pass.

"Wendy and I would pool all our money and buy whatever second-hand parts we could," Graeme recalls. "We put the supercharged engine together with direct drive and the diff from an F100 and ran the quickest time ever at that date.

"Wendy owned 50 per cent of everything then and she still owns 50 per cent of everything now. She's my best friend and my biggest backer, and I couldn't have done anything without her support."

Next came Psycho III, which in 1973 became the first Fuel Altered in Australia to run 200mph.

"That took all our dedication and money," says Graeme. "I was a truck driver and Wendy was a clerk, and we used to work as much overtime as we could to get the funds to buy the parts, and then spent all weekend and every night working on the car."

The Cowins then bought into a speed shop business and in time were able to fund their incredible adventures through the business and its later offshoots, Rocket Industries and Aeroflow.

The Cowins moved from altereds into a series of Nitro Funny Cars. Each pushed the envelope; in 1978, their Camaro became the first Australian Funny Car into the sixes, and in 1986, their Trans Am was the first into the fives.

They took the Trans Am to the US in 1985 and were immediately competitive, qualifying for the US Nationals at Indianapolis to face John Force in the first round. In 1987, Graeme made it all the way to the final of the Winternationals, bowing out to the Budweiser-backed Kenny Bernstein.

Back in Australia, Graeme moved to Top Fuel and quickly came to grips with it, running the first four-second pass outside the USA, a 4.89@294mph in 1993 at Calder Park. In 1995, Cowin won the Australian Top Fuel Championship, the Triple Challenge at Eastern Creek, the Winternationals and the Grand Finals – all in the one year! He then won the Winternationals again in 1997 and the '98 Nationals, as well as scoring an all-time Australian low ET of 4.81 seconds. The original car crashed at Calder during the '94 Nationals, and its replacement was bent at Willowbank in June 1998 after it sheared the studs on one rear wheel and nailed the concrete wall. That was the end of Graeme's driving career.

Sons Andrew and John also competed at the highest levels of Top Fuel, with Andrew making the finals of the US Nationals in 1999 and finishing 11th in the 2001 NHRA Top Fuel Championship after competing in just 15 out of 23 rounds.

Back in Australia in 2002, Andrew ran the first-ever 500km/h pass outside of the US, resetting the Australian ET record to 4.75 seconds and recording the first-ever side-by-side four-second pass on Australian soil. John won the Australian Top Fuel Championship for 2003-'04.

In 2013, Graeme and Wendy returned to their Funny Car roots and created the Aeroflow Outlaw Nitro Funny Car series, building a stable of nostalgia nitro floppers that tour the country to this day.

For his services to the sport, Graeme was inducted into the Don Garlits Museum of Drag Racing Hall of Fame in 2023.

MIDDLE LEFT: Graeme and Wendy have owned a few hot street cars, but none more famous than King Kong 'Cuda, which won the 2010 Street Machine of the Year gong

LEFT: The Cowin & Johns Mustang was the couple's first Funny Car, seen here at Castlereagh International Dragway in 1974

OPPOSITE PAGE: The Cowins have been running the Aeroflow Outlaw Nitro Funny Car Series since 2013, building an impressive fleet of 13 nostalgia-style cars that tour the country. Last year, they returned to competition drag racing at the top level with a Toyota-bodied car to run in 400 Thunder's new Top Fuel Funny Car class

STORY DAVID COOK **PHOTOS** PETER BATEMAN & *SM* ARCHIVES

Cowin Mustang

Psycho II

Top Fueler

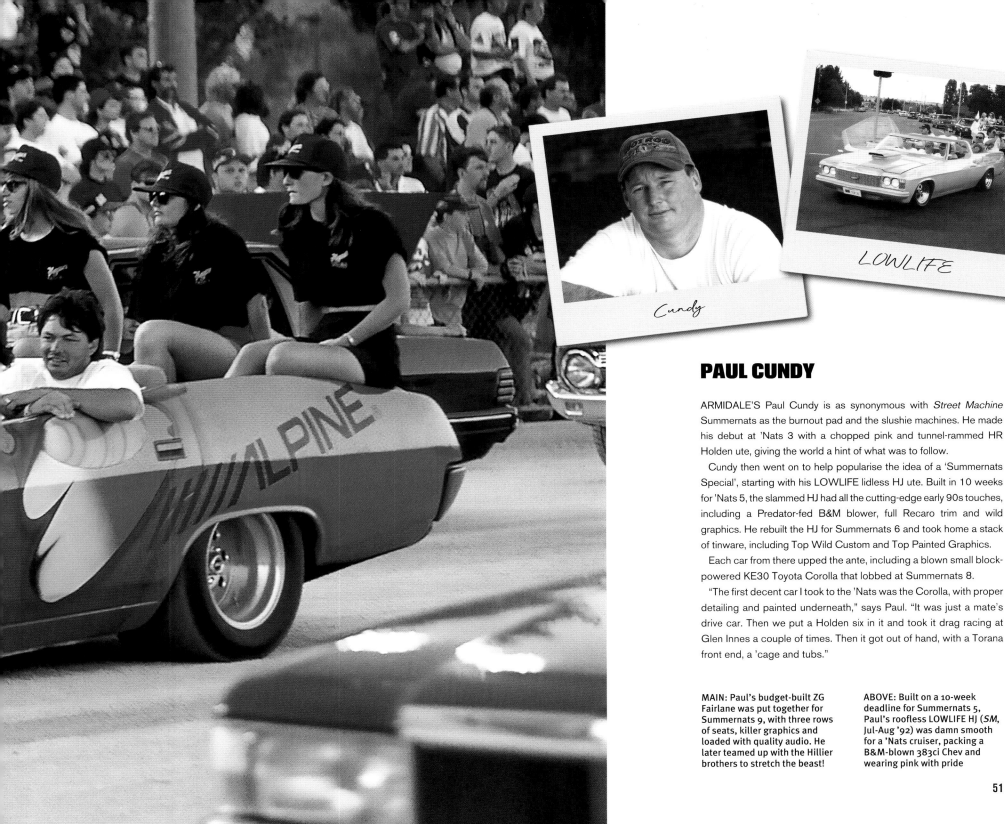

LOWLIFE

Cundy

PAUL CUNDY

ARMIDALE'S Paul Cundy is as synonymous with *Street Machine* Summernats as the burnout pad and the slushie machines. He made his debut at 'Nats 3 with a chopped pink and tunnel-rammed HR Holden ute, giving the world a hint of what was to follow.

Cundy then went on to help popularise the idea of a 'Summernats Special', starting with his LOWLIFE lidless HJ ute. Built in 10 weeks for 'Nats 5, the slammed HJ had all the cutting-edge early 90s touches, including a Predator-fed B&M blower, full Recaro trim and wild graphics. He rebuilt the HJ for Summernats 6 and took home a stack of tinware, including Top Wild Custom and Top Painted Graphics.

Each car from there upped the ante, including a blown small block-powered KE30 Toyota Corolla that lobbed at Summernats 8.

"The first decent car I took to the 'Nats was the Corolla, with proper detailing and painted underneath," says Paul. "It was just a mate's drive car. Then we put a Holden six in it and took it drag racing at Glen Innes a couple of times. Then it got out of hand, with a Torana front end, a 'cage and tubs."

MAIN: Paul's budget-built ZG Fairlane was put together for Summernats 9, with three rows of seats, killer graphics and loaded with quality audio. He later teamed up with the Hillier brothers to stretch the beast!

ABOVE: Built on a 10-week deadline for Summernats 5, Paul's roofless LOWLIFE HJ (*SM*, Jul-Aug '92) was damn smooth for a 'Nats cruiser, packing a B&M-blown 383ci Chev and wearing pink with pride

51

ZG Fairlane stretch

Arguably the pinnacle of the Summernats Specials was Paul's ZG Fairlane. Like the HJ, the roof was removed, but this time an extra row of seats was added for maximum party, matched to batshit-crazy graphics and an over-the-top stereo system, as was the style of the time. He later teamed up with the Hillier brothers to stretch the ZG to accommodate even more party animals.

Decades later, you can bet that most years Paul will lob at Summernats in some outrageous ride and spend the weekend having a fat time with his mates.

Perhaps all of this was inevitable, as Paul is the son of Aussie vanning royalty (his dad is Doug Cundy of Mystic Illusions XY Falcon fame), and he went to TAFE to learn panel beating alongside future next-level metal man Clayton Hillier.

Paul has had a hand in a stack of top-shelf streeters over the years, including Jason 'Dick' Tracey's stunning FJ (*SM*, Sep '03) and Dean Wilson's MYDADS '37 Plymouth coupe (*SM Hot Rod* 20).

MIDDLE LEFT: Cundy created this yellow-with-graphics '76 Corolla (*SM*, Mar '95) with a tube frame, big tubs, 9in diff and tower-of-power V8. It was featured in overseas mags, gave the 1995 SMOTY award a solid nudge, and was then sold and remade into a rotary-powered drag car

LEFT: Built from a lowly VB SL and converted to VK sheet metal, Cundy's Commodore (*SM*, Feb '01) was too smooth

for words. Highlights included a beautifully integrated VR-style dash and trim and a mega-smooth engine bay holding a 332ci donk

OPPOSITE PAGE: Paul's latest is this EJ Holden ute, bought locally from a deceased estate, complete with super-rad old-school canopy. A lowering job, a set of Tasman mags and some cool signwriting resulted in another instant classic

STORY GLENN TORRENS **PHOTOS** *SM* ARCHIVES

MY DADS coupe

Cundy cruisin'

Armidale WINDSCREENS

Major Tom

JOHN EVANS

VANNING godfather John Evans has had a hand in more iconic Aussie car culture moments than most of us could dream of.

John emigrated from England in 1956, but not before a visit to Colin Chapman's Lotus factory lit his five-year-old mind aflame. The family landed in Dandenong, and as a teenager John became smitten with both drag racing and surfing.

In 1971, a job signwriting for Kevin Dennis Motors saw John get a deal on one of the first HQ vans built, complete with 308, four-speed and GTS goodies. Initially, John decked out the living quarters to make his surf trips more comfortable, but a desire for individuality saw him turn the HQ into Tangerine Dream, considered by most historians to be the OG custom van.

Along with David Baird of Igloo HQ fame, John formed the Victorian Panel Van Club in 1974 and the scene snowballed.

"By then I was working for a design company called Graf-X International, working on everything from Brock Toranas to the *Mad Max* '59 Chev and vans aplenty," says John. "When I discovered airbrushing through the US *Truckin'* mag and picked up an airbrush, it all came together."

Tangerine Dream II

John Evans, centre, of Van Makers Aust. checks the interior with the Chrysler men who are obviously happy with their new addition to the Valiant range.

ABOVE: The original Tangerine Dream was T-boned and then rebodied in black as Reincarnation. It was then taken back to orange as Tangerine Dream II in '77. A sponsorship deal from Cheviot saw John develop his Manta kit to cover the 10in Hotwires

TOP LEFT: The success of the white Coca-Cola 3XY Freedom Machine Bedford built at Vanmakers Australia paved the way for three black versions built by John and the crew at Vancraft. The Freedom Machine name was retained for the NSW and WA versions, while the Victorian van was called Easy Roller

BOTTOM LEFT: "The VU Sandman build was all top-secret stuff with the factory in lockdown – we even slept on-site," John says. "It didn't matter, though, as we felt like part of something huge"

After Graf-X and a spell at Vanmakers Australia, John and a partner formed Vancraft, a dedicated van shop that had a staff of 10. Output included John Skilbeck's Hallucination XB, Mark Simons's Wrest Point HJ, and the Bush Beast 4x4 Bedford for BF Goodrich.

John's reputation made the manufacturers take notice, with both Holden and Chrysler seeking his input prior to the release of the HX Sandman and Drifter, respectively.

When the van craze waned in the early 80s, John and wife Lucy started Stylestripe Customs, which morphed into Racepaint in 1991. John's post-van work included contract jobs for GM-H, bikes, speedboats, Eric Bana's XB, many *Street Machine* feature cars and hundreds of fibreglass Ronald McDonald statues!

Things came full circle in 2000 when Holden came knocking once more, recruiting Racepaint to do the panel and paint on the VU Sandman show car.

John has now stepped back from the business to enjoy retirement, with son David at the helm.

STORY SIMON MAJOR **PHOTOS** CRISTIAN BRUNELLI & *SM* ARCHIVES

Easy Roller

John built the Freedom Roller Bedford in 2014 for mate Don Hailes as a tribute to the 3XY Freedom Machine and Easy Roller giveaway vans

57

FOR SALE
58 2737

58

PETER FITZPATRICK

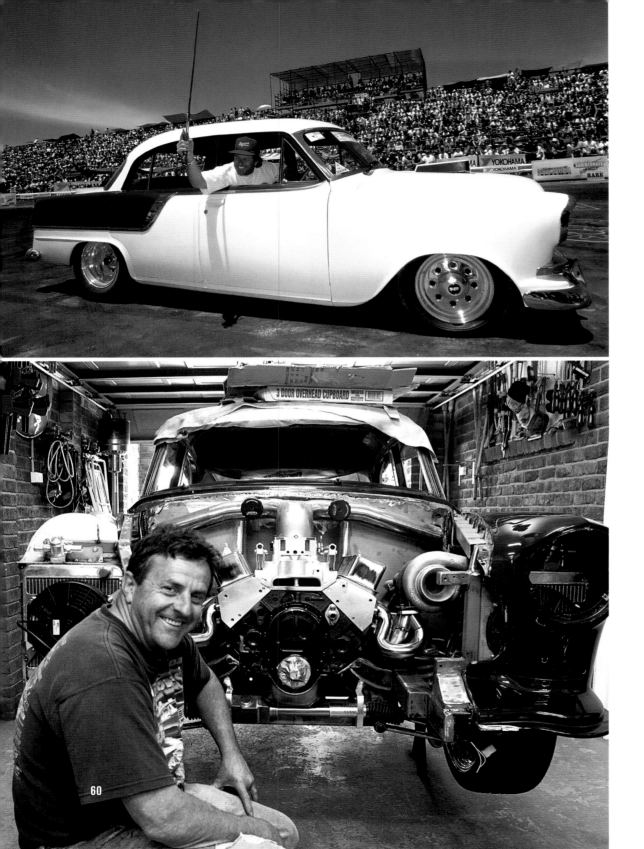

UNDISPUTED SIX-TIME CHAMP

THERE aren't many guys who were at the very first Street Machine Nationals in 1975 who are still active at the pointy end of our sport, but Canberra's Peter Fitzpatrick sure is.

Fitzy won Top Engine Bay at the first Nationals, held in Griffith, with what he calls his first serious car, an EH Holden.

"It had a 192 with triple SUs and a drag-spec Bert Jones 40/80 cam," he says. "It only had a three-speed, but it ran flat 15s at Castlereagh and would do 100mph in second gear. I broke a lot of second-gear synchros and diffs.

"At that first Nationals, I won a socket set and four litres of oil. But would you believe I never got the trophy? They said they were going to get it engraved with my name and send it to me. I'm still waiting."

Peter sold the EH after it started attracting the attention of too many police and used the money to buy an HK Brougham he called Broomstick. "I pulled the 307 out of it, took it out to 327, put some big heads on it and a Muncie behind it," he says. "I got it up to 6300rpm in top, which is probably about 155mph. It ran flat 13s with 3.08 gears, but on the highway it was untouchable. You could flatten it at 120mph and it would put you back in your seat."

Fitzy put around 300 hours into the bodywork of the HK, pumped out the rear guards to accommodate the 11-inch rear rubber, and resprayed the lot in Glacier White.

"This was my first real show/comp car," Peter says. "I built it as a tidy street car, then later when I'd seen what others were doing to the undersides of their cars, I came back and detailed the undercarriage."

The car that really made his name was his wife Michelle's FC Holden. It was her first car, in fact, bought for $240 out of *The Canberra Times*.

PREVIOUS PAGES (58-59):
Peter's Brougham was an absolute show-and-go grunter. Tough enough, in fact, to score a win against John Peterson's Zephyr in the Go-to-Whoa at an early Street Machine Nationals

LEFT: At home in the shed, mid-Trilogy build. The way Fitzy integrated the mirror-image turbos and PWR intercoolers into the third iteration of the FC was next-level

TOP LEFT: Build number one of wife Michelle's FC Holden saw Fitzy take out four Grand Champion swords at *Street Machine* Summernats

TOP RIGHT: Twelve months after a prang at Summernats 2000, Fitzy had rebuilt the FC and given it a white-on-blue makeover. The car took out People's Choice at Summernats in 2001, and Peter returned with it the next year to win his fifth Grand Champion gong

FC original

FC phase II

FC Trilogy

61

'35 Chev at SEMA

OPPOSITE PAGE: The '35 Chev coupe that Peter built for Kees Weel won the GM Design Award at the 2019 SEMA Show

RIGHT: Both Peter's sons are also heavily into cars and are fans of Japanese metal. Aaron built a ProCharged SR20-powered Datsun 1600 to an elite standard, taking out People's Choice and Grand Champion at Summernats in 2006

BOTTOM RIGHT: Fitz bought his '34 after it had been severely damaged by an engine bay fire, devastating then-owner Gary Reid. Peter took the remains off Gary's hands and rebuilt it into flash cruiser with a distinct old-school vibe

The FItzpatricks used it as daily transport until it was pulled off the road in 1987 for a tidy-up – one that got massively out of control. The desire to have both fat rubber and V8 power within the confines of the law necessitated a three-quarter HQ chassis and floorpan graft.

A stack of subtle body mods, trick blue-on-white duco, and impressive detailing saw the car win four *Street Machine* Summernats Grand Champion gongs between 1993 and 1999.

An argument with the Armco on the Summernats Go-to-Whoa pad in 2000 prompted rebuild number two. This time Fitzy reversed the colour scheme to white-on-blue, and gave the interior a total revamp, including a false flat floor and a stack of top-level car audio.

He returned to the 'Nats in 2001 and took out People's Choice, and followed up in 2002 with his fifth Grand Champ win.

Son Aaron also managed both feats in 2006 with his Datsun 1600, before Peter returned with the third incarnation of the FC in 2011. This one was the biggie, with a twin-turbo 440-cube small-block under the bonnet, all-new underpinnings, wild candy green paint and much more.

The car debuted at MotorEx 2010 and won the Car of the Decade award. At Summernats in 2011, it made a clean sweep of the big three gongs, winning People's Choice, Grand Champion and Top Judged in one hit. A Street Machine of the Year win naturally followed.

Peter himself was also named a Rare Spares Legend and was awarded Master Craftsman status at Summernats 35 in 2023.

Since then, he's built himself a bad-arse '34 coupe, worked with his sons to put a new spin on the Howard Astill-built ROCK 4 Compact Fairlane, and knocked up an incredible '35 Chev coupe with Corvette underpinnings for PWR's Kees Weel.

Pete has been giving us running updates on how his new project (still under wraps, sorry) has been going, and it doesn't sound like his enthusiasm for the sport has dimmed at all since 1975.

STORY SIMON TELFORD **PHOTOS** *SM* ARCHIVES

SMOTY *winner*

ALAN FLEMING

THE glory days of the Australian van craze were over by the time Alan Fleming's Motorvator dropped like an alien spacecraft into the Aussie show scene at the start of the 1990s. Pro streeters now ruled the roost, and Alan's HG van-meets-VK Calais creation had precisely zero in common with those drag-inspired weapons.

When the HG appeared on the April-May 1990 cover of *SM* with the cover line 'Loony Bin', the VK front end and tail-lights weren't the craziest parts of the build. After all, Aussies had been updating their rides with later-model looks for at least a couple of decades by that point. No, what was really wild was the concept, Alan dreaming up a world where Holden built a high-roof sports van as a true 2+2, with long Monaro doors for both style and practicality and extra-long pillarless side glass so the rear passengers could enjoy the view.

It was a great idea – and one that we wish Holden had built – but Alan wanted much more. What he delivered was a concept car, removing all trace of the 1960s styling and producing something akin to a commercial vehicle hyped up to compete in the IMSA GTO ranks of the day. This was achieved by pumping out the bodywork with flares and side skirts to cover wide Simmons rims – 15x10 inches at the front and 15x12 at the rear – and matching Pirelli rubber.

You could fill a book with the neat tricks Alan employed to contemporise the HG, but suffice to say they include a tapered roof chop, flush-fitting glass, concealed wipers, widened VK bumpers and the insane custom tailgate.

TOP LEFT: Alan's Extra FX model range includes coupe, drop-top and roadster pick-up takes on Australia's Own. Look up 'Ffx/ffj' on Facebook for more info

ABOVE: Alan hasn't been idle since Motorvator. His J-Rod was an audacious concept using late-model Commodore suspension and driveline

Just as Alan eschewed the sword-and-saucy-maiden murals of the show van era on the outside, he also gave the traditional sin-bin interior a big swerve. Four Recaro buckets, grey velour and polished wood gave the inside a much more contemporary vibe.

And as if the van itself wasn't innovative enough, consider Alan's approach to securing sponsorship for the HG's second build, which we featured in *SM*, June 1991. The first step was his choice of stark white duco for the original build, leaving a blank canvas for any future sponsor. The second was to buy a suit for his meeting with the good folks at Dulux. Alan reckons he never wore it again, but it helped seal a deal that saw the van become the Dulux Motorvator, complete with jaw-dropping multi-colour paintwork.

Alan had plans for big-block Chev power and mega wheel tubs to replace the comparably tame 308 drivetrain. However, he busied himself with his J-Rod and more recent Extra FX FFX/FFJ concepts, so the Motorvator stayed untouched.

But after many years in storage, the van has recently seen the light of day, now owned by Alan's nephew Grant Fleming. It's still in remarkably good condition considering its age, and there are plans afoot to revive the van and return it to the public arena. We cannot wait!

STORY SIMON MAJOR & SIMON TELFORD
PHOTOS GARTSIDE & PETER BATEMAN

Dulux Motorvator

Alan Fleming

Dulux MOTORVATOR

Along with Victor Bray's '57 and John Zappia's HQ, Ben's XA coupe is among the most iconic local drag racing sedans ever and was a major player in the explosion of Top Doorslammer racing

Gatt brothers

Super Flow Heads

BEN & JOE GATT

IF CHEV fans had Victor Bray as their hero, Ford guys and gals had Joe and Ben Gatt. Their careers as rodders, racers and go-fast gurus spanned from the earliest days of the sport, through to the birth of the Wild Bunch and beyond.

The boys were born in Malta and were only little kids when the family settled in the Sydney suburb of Fairfield in 1950. Their dad Paulo was a car guy, and the lads were pulling apart and rebuilding engines under his watchful eye long before they were of legal driving age.

By 1963, at the tender ages of 19 and 16, respectively, Ben and Joe became founding members of the Gladiators Hot Rod Club. Joe had just bought what was to become his first real hot rod, a '34 coupe. At this very early moment in our sport, hot rodding and drag racing were one and the same.

The brothers got their first look at real drag competition that year, driving all the way to Melbourne to witness the Big Go South at Melbourne's Riverside strip. The fire was lit, and after giving racing a go at Sydney's newly launched Castlereagh, the boys returned to Riverside to compete in the first Drag Racing Nationals in 1965.

TOP LEFT: Joe's first proper race car was a Y-block-powered '34 coupe, which competed in front of 10,000 fans at the very first Nationals at Riverside in 1965. Twenty-six years later, the boys won the Nationals in Ben's XA

ABOVE: Ben's first racer was this Model A bucket, seen here at the 1967 Mr Holden event at Castlereagh

LEFT: After running a flathead-powered dragster for a time, the boys moved into sedans, first with this FX Holden and then into a lighter Anglia – both with Y-block power

BOTTOM LEFT: The Capri Nitro Funny Car was a major step up, first with an injected 427 Ford and then a blown 329 Hemi. Ben came runner-up at the '74 Nationals, won the '75 Summernationals, and ran as quick as 8.22 seconds at 191mph before it was destroyed in a fire at AIR

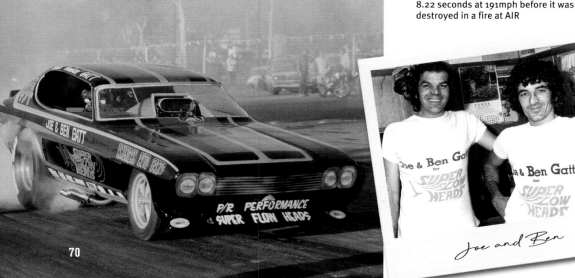

Joe and Ben

With Joe's '34 coupe kitted out with a 272 Y-block, the brothers towed it to Melbourne using an A-bar set-up on what was then a 20-hour drive on appalling roads.

Despite being knocked out by John English's iconic '32 roadster in the quarter-finals of eliminations, the roar of the 10,000-strong crowd and the hype of big-time racing had both boys hooked.

Joe built a sidevalve dragster but gave it up when he married. He instead directed his energy into founding a new business, Super Flow Heads. Ben, by now a fanatical racer, soon joined him there. Joe became his bro's crew chief.

Ben's racing career touched on all of the most exciting genres. He became embroiled in the gasser wars of the late 60s and early 70s in his FX Holden and Anglia; went full-tilt into the early days of Nitro Funny Cars; enjoyed the glory days of Super Stock; and, finally, the crowd-pleasing fury of the Wild Bunch and Top Doorslammer.

Of all their cars, Ben's favourite remains the XA Falcon hardtop that he still races today. His career highlight came in April 1991, when he drove the XA to a Super Stock win at the Nationals. It was also a big moment for Joe, who'd been trying to win that meeting since that 1965 race at Riverside.

Joe's favourite car was their EA Falcon Top Doorslammer, which became the quickest Ford in the world with a 6.67 in 1995 and remains in the family today.

The team raced at every track in Australia bar Darwin, toured New Zealand, and were away racing as many as 30 weekends a year, transporting car and crew in the team's famous bus.

As Joe's son Warren recalls: "I know winning the Nationals was pretty big for Dad, but I think building the bus was his biggest success. It used to be a convoy of cars when they went racing, but with the bus everyone could be together. That's what he always wanted, for the family to be together in racing."

Both Ben and Joe returned to their street car roots in the early-2000s. Joe built a slick '32 roadster, and Ben, a wild Lincoln Zephyr and a chopped Mercury.

Joe passed away on 3 December 2014, aged 73. Ben continues to race and recently completed a restoration of dad Paulo's long-lost XT Falcon.

STORY PETER BATEMAN & DAVE COOK
PHOTOS PETER BATEMAN & *SM* ARCHIVES

EASTERN CREEK

Joe's F.E.D. '69

C/GAS Capri, '83

Ben's Lincoln Zephyr

TORCO

TORCO HI-VIZ
SYNTHETIC RACING OIL

SUPER FLOW HEADS

The pinnacle of the Gatts' Top
Doorslammer ambitions was the
428 Shotgun-powered EA Falcon,
which was, for a time, the quickest
Ford Doorslammer in the world

Steve Athans's Mustang

72

GEORGE HADDAD

BASED in Dandenong, Victoria, Haddad Race Cars & Engines has been famous nationwide for crazy engines and fast cars for decades. Run by George Haddad and his brother Ray, the passion for racing and learning has alway set them apart from the pack.

Ray and George arrived in Australia at the ages of 15 and 12, respectively, and, without much English, left school early.

"I left school in Year 9 and had a few different jobs, and Ray went to work with Dad as a diesel fitter," says George. "I never had to touch an engine until 1984, even though I'd started racing cars. Then Ray went on holiday and I thought I'd give it a go.

"I worked at a few different shops and learnt a lot there, including Rod City Repros, COME, and Graeme Withers Speed Shop. You don't have to be Einstein to do this; just practice and figure out your own way of doing things."

After racing a variety of cars and developing a taste for nitrous, the boys put together a gassed 308-powered Capri in the late 80s, that wore McCreary street rubber and ran flat 10s. But their next Capri really made people stand up and pay attention, being the first in the world to run eights on street rubber.

"It had a 500ci Chev, and went 8.92 with a shot of gas at Calder," says George. "We got a fair amount of attention for that, so I thought I'd have a go at doing it for a living."

Aside from a short stint running a pizza shop, the Haddads have been building engines and helping folks go fast ever since, including Pro Street legends Steve Athans and Craig Gerdes.

Through it all, street cars have remained George's passion. "When Calder was pumping, we'd drive down there every Friday night, which is about an hour from here in the traffic," he says. "We put a race number on the car and race, then wipe the number off and drive home. It's no good saying that the car runs 9.30s but you have to change this or change that to drive it."

STORY SIMON TELFORD **PHOTOS** PETER BATEMAN & *SM* ARCHIVES

ABOVE: George's Capri (*SM*, Apr/May '93) was the first car on earth to run eights on street rubber

LEFT: George has done some cool one-off jobs, including building and setting up the twin-blown EFI Boss 429 engine in Rod Hadfield's Grandma Duck T-coupe

BELOW: After a running a monster turbo SBF in his XR Falcon, George went back to aspirated form a few years ago and has a ball competing at Drag Challenge events

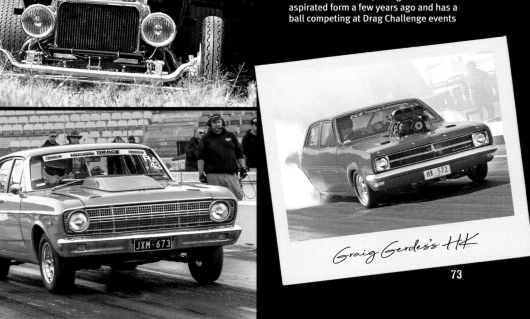

Graig Gerdes's HK

The Warman Special

ROD HADFIELD

'34 coupe

Blown MkII Zephyr

MAD SCIENTIST

LOOK, Rod Hadfield wasn't the first guy to build a hot rod in Australia – not by a long shot – but he is undoubtedly one of the most prolific and consistently innovative builders in the country. Add to that the groundbreaking work that he and wife Carol have done to advance the modified car industry – plus their efforts both on and off the salt flats at Lake Gairdner – and you've got yourself a legend of significant proportions.

Born in 1946, Rod left school at 14 to work on the family farm in Stanhope, Victoria. He had a fascination with machinery and vehicles and by 15 had built a rudimentary T-bucket from scavenged bits and pieces.

His next build, however, was far from basic – a blown '34 Ford coupe. After a five-year build, it won Top Coupe on debut at the 1967 Melbourne Hot Rod Show – incredible stuff from a bucks-down farm boy with zero training or access to the parts and services we now take for granted.

Having conquered the world of hot rods, Rod took on the nascent street machine scene with a 1956 MkII Zephyr that he repowered with a blown and injected small-block Chev – to our knowledge the first such car built in Australia.

By 1975, Rod had fled the farm and he and Carol had moved their young family to Castlemaine, already established as the epicentre of street rod activity Down Under. Rod had a mini sideline gig making gearbox conversion kits for Holdens, but after running his first advertisement in *Custom Rodder* in December 1975, interest exploded from across the country and the Castlemaine Rod Shop was born.

PREVIOUS PAGES (74-75): The Warman Special (*SM*, Mar '10) is a full-size version of a stainless-steel model built by Rod's grandfather Ray 'Pa' Warman. Pa Warman was a pivotal figure in Rod's life who supported and encouraged the young man's obsession with cars

FAR LEFT: The Redback 1948 Anglia featured a blown small-block, clutched TH400 and chop top. The car debuted in 1977 and remains in the collection unchanged

LEFT: Rod and Carol have tackled many ambitious projects, including the CRS 'Rodent' big-block, which was to be used for the small aircraft industry, as well as racing. Red tape and funding woes killed an idea that was ahead of its time

OPPOSITE PAGE: Rod's twin-blown Boss 429-powered T-model coupe (*SM*, Jun '98) was a mindblowing car in its day and remains a stand-out. You can check it out at Hadfield's Hot Rods in Chewton, Victoria

EK couch

Chevy C10

Hot Rod Lincoln

Fire CHIEF

AMERICAN LA FRANCE

ATTACK

Walk the Line '32 coupe

78

RIGHT: The Final Objective '55 Chevy (*SM*, Apr '03) was perhaps Rod's most audacious build and was recognised as the World's Most Powerful Street-Registered car by Guinness World Records

BELOW RIGHT: Rod has pursued land speed racing with vigour since the first DLRA meeting on Lake Gairdner in 1990. He was the first to join the organisation's 200 MPH Club in the Salt Shaker dragster, then went on to race the Bronze Aussie Commodore in Australia and a Studebaker at Bonneville in the US

OPPOSITE PAGE: Rod loves stuffing giant engines into tiny cars, including a 572ci American LaFrance V12 into a 1948 Fiat Topolino, dubbed Fire Chief and featured in *SM Hot Rod* 18

By the time the couple sold the business in 2004, the Rod Shop had manufactured more than 2000 product lines and Rod had built dozens of cars, both for personal expression and to showcase the company's wares.

Once free from the constraints of shop life, the Hadfields shipped three of Rod's most audacious creations to the US – the Rolls-Royce Merlin-powered Final Objective '55 Chevy, the twin-blown Model T coupe, and the Hot Rod Lincoln pick-up as their driver. They took a year to tour the motherland, ticking experiences off their bucket lists while the cars collected trophies at events like the Grand National Roadster Show, Goodguys and the Super Chevy Show. Adventures included meeting a who's who of American hot rodding legends (think George Barris and Tommy Ivo for starters) and having the pick-up used in a Cindy Crawford photoshoot!

The '55 was sold in the US, and, when they returned to Australia, Rod got busy building his man cave, an 860-plus square-metre shed with half the floor space devoted to housing the car collection and the other half a workshop. Rod is now able to build his dreams away from the pressures of business, although he and Carol have continued with two smaller concerns: Stubtech drop axles, and a more boutique operation fabricating '33-'34 Ford grilles.

Even with the demands of keeping a business and a production line of epic car builds running, Rod and Carol have devoted considerable time and energy to organisations like the Dry Lakes Racers Australia and the Castlemaine Hot Rod Centre for the good of all enthusiasts.

STORY SIMON TELFORD **PHOTOS** *SM* ARCHIVES

Chic in '86

Mr Summernats

CHIC HENRY 1946-2022

Chic and Georgia

HIS DREAM IS OUR REALITY

IF *STREET Machine* is the bible of our sport, then Summernats must be Christmas, Bathurst and the Olympics all rolled into one. There are stacks of great automotive events on offer around the country these days, but the Summernats remains the biggest, wildest and most diverse of them all. And the bloke we have to thank for it is the late Anthony Robert 'Chic' Henry.

Chic grew up in Tasmania, and after serving in the army in Melbourne, Sydney and Townsville, he returned to civilian life in Brisbane in 1973. It wasn't long before he was up to his neck in the primordial stew of the town's hot-car scene.

"I worked at Surfers Paradise Raceway as a scrutineer for seven years, but I was caught between hot rodding, drag racing and this new street machine thing," Chic told *SM* in an interview for the January 2022 issue. "The fact that I owned a '57 Chev meant I was accepted by the hot rodders. I loved the drags but also liked the street aspect, and people like myself were starting to form clubs for these 'late-model' cars."

Across the country, the street machine scene was starting to get organised, and when the first Street Machine Nationals was held in 1975, Chic was entrant number one. The various states began to pool resources, with Chic representing Queensland to work with Dave Ryan from Victoria and Rowan Wilson from New South Wales to stage the fourth Street Machine Nationals in Narrandera in 1980.

"By the time we got to Narrandera, I had worked out what I wanted to do with my life," said Chic. "I wanted to drive my tough street car whenever I could. I liked to drag race it from time to time and put it into shows whenever I wanted. I enjoyed hanging out, *American Graffiti*-style.

TOP LEFT: After finding his footing with a hot EH and even hotter slant-six Valiant, Chic discovered that his true love was big Chevys. It started with a '57 before he found the automotive love of his life, a '62 Chevrolet Super Sport, shot here at the old Brisbane Museum for the fourth issue of *SM*, Apr-May '82

BOTTOM LEFT: "I met Rick Dobbertin at the Street Machine Nationals in Du Quoin, Illinois," recalled Chic. "There were

a lot of great cars there, but it was clear Rick's Pontiac was head-and-shoulders. I had no trouble convincing him to bring it to Australia for the first Summernats. Then I just had to make it happen"

OPPOSITE PAGE: Chic had a long-running column in *SM* for many years, appropriately dubbed Shooting the Breeze, and he featured in many *SM* photoshoots, including this cracker by Peter Bateman

On the tools for SM

Bus pull, 'Nats 10

Lawrence Legend

OPPOSITE PAGE: Chic liked to up the ante with crazy stunts, like daredevil Lawrence Legend's epic bus jumps. At Summernats 9, a Leyland P76 met a monster truck. The following year, we got the bus pull

RIGHT: For many years, Chic and the '62 opened the burnout competition. Dig the quad-Weber set-up from Summernats 1!

BELOW RIGHT: Chic scored his first-ever *SM* cover shot when his Camaro caught fire at Summernats 21. His wife Debra was aboard for her first and last time riding shotgun on the pad

BOTTOM RIGHT: While it's hard to imagine Summernats without a Grand Champion, the award wasn't introduced until 1993. "We wanted to come up with something different, which led to the Grand Champion, harking back to the medieval tournaments before the king and queen," explained Chic. "The champion was the knight who took on all comers, so that's the Grand Champion who gets the sword"

"Narrandera was the start of the states working together, so from there we created a national organisation, the Australian Street Machine Federation. I became the national director. The Street Machine Nationals had outgrown the smaller country towns, so we moved it to Canberra and ran it there in '82, '84 and '86."

Inspired by his visits to the US Street Machine Nationals in both Tulsa and Du Quoin, Chic thought the Australian version could be turned into something incredible, so he moved to Canberra to devote himself to the cause. But not everyone shared his vision.

"For '87, I put a proposal to the ASMF to run the Nationals as a satellite to the Federation," Chic explained. "They couldn't agree, so I approached *Street Machine* to be the major sponsor and we staged the first Summernats in 1988."

Chic's formula for success was to take the Street Machine Nationals and enhance it, adding special attractions each year.

"It was important to add pure spectacle to the proceedings," said Chic. "The biggest compliment was when people would ask, 'What have you got planned for next year, Chic?' That's why I kept looking for new and wilder things to feature, working with guys like Lawrence Legend to amp it up each time."

Chic drove it like Brocky until 2009, when he sold the event to new owners Andy Lopez, Dom McCormack and Andrew Bee. Right until the end, Chic remained involved, crowning each new Grand Champion and moving among his flock.

"I know how much Summernats means to so many people; it's their Mecca, which pleases me enormously," said Chic. "I'm so grateful to all those people who came to my party and enjoyed it with me."

STORY SIMON TELFORD **PHOTOS** *SM* ARCHIVES

Camaro fire, 'Nats 21

Chic with Troy Trepanier

XP cruiser

Hillier brothers

EA ute

TROY & CLAYTON HILLIER

BROTHERS Troy and Clayton Hillier turn out some of the most exquisitely crafted hearses made anywhere in the world at their day gig, Hillier by Design Coachbuilding, based in Tenterfield. But in their downtime, the boys have been known to employ their skills to build some of the most memorable and innovative Blue Oval-based street machines around.

"The fun began with my old white XP Falcon that I took to Summernats in the mid-90s," says Troy. "I'd raced cars for years, Minis mostly, but I got sick of repairing race cars, so I looked for something else and found modified cars.

"After the white car, we built an EA Falcon ute. That was what got us noticed, I reckon, because it was totally factory-looking, but was a car that didn't exist from the factory. People didn't realise what they were looking at.

"Then there was the Tiger Mica XP hardtop, the green AU two-door, another red two-door Falcon, the Arrow, the Raptor, a green XP Falcon cruiser. That was my favourite; I wish I still had it. Oh yeah, Clayton's got a dual-cab AU ute, too. And we stretched Paul Cundy's ZG Fairlane cruiser."

Rovera AU coupe

TOP LEFT & ABOVE: The boys built three stunning AU coupes that looked so near to factory jobs it wasn't funny. The first one debuted at Summernats 13 in 2000, and was later reborn as the blown 4.6L quad-cam AEC 300+ shown here

LEFT: The third AU coupe build was the wild Arrow hardtop, done in cooperation with Recaro and MOMO specialist Roman Auto-Tek. It runs a Clayton-built 6.3L mill

OPPOSITE PAGE: Commissioned by Roman Auto-Tek, Raptor was a BA XR6 ute with hydraulic gullwing doors that was hot enough to star in a Tooheys beer ad

It's an impressive résumé, racked up in just over a decade, but what's really mindblowing is how the lads combine their technical prowess with flat-out style. With the XP hardops, they proved they could build stunners at both the extreme and the streetable levels.

The Hilliers' repeated success in turning near-new Falcons into body styles that the factory never built was so impressive that Ford Australia eventually came knocking. Working with Advanced Engine Components and Millard Design, Ford turned the lads' AU coupe into the mighty 300+, which wowed the crowds at the 2001 Melbourne Motor Show.

As their hearse business has continued to grow – including partnerships with European hearse manufacturers to bring in some wild Mercedes and Jaguar-based creations – the boys have been quiet on the show scene, but word is they've been cooking up something new in their spare time, and it's not a Ford! Still, you can bet it'll blow minds.

STORY GLENN TORRENS **PHOTOS** SIMON DAVIDSON & *SM* ARCHIVES

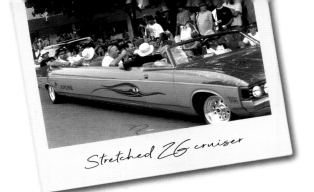

Stretched ZG cruiser

Clayton's AU Crewman

Obsession '37 roadster

ABOVE & RIGHT: Paul was called upon by hot rodder Peter Elliot to design and build his wildly innovative, MotorEx Best of Breed-winning '37 Ford roadster dubbed Obsession (*SM*, May '08). Paul later worked his magic on Peter's Simplicity '34 Ford tudor (*SM Hot Rod* 17)

Simplicity '34 tudor

PAUL KELLY

OF ALL the genres that *Street Machine* covers, that of the traditional custom would have to be the most rarefied. While customs were Australia's first mainstream car craze, the scene was starting to wane when a young Paul Kelly was learning his trades in the 1970s. Panel vans, street machines and resto rods ruled the roost, and, while Paul worked on them all, he never lost his love for the true custom.

Born in Sydney, 10-year-old Paul's addiction to *Custom Rodder* led him to the doorstep of Jeff Dellow, who, besides being a founder of that esteemed magazine, was a founding member of the Romans Hot Rod Club, and later the man behind conversion kings Dellow Automotive. Paul hung around and was eventually taught the basics of welding and fabrication. After three years as an apprentice motor mechanic, he switched to spray painting and badgered the older guys to teach him panel beating.

This was the era of Brickies and Big Chief's, and Paul was in the thick of it with a succession of hot Holdens, humpy and otherwise.

By the 80s he was chopping roofs, doing factory-style convertible jobs, airbrushing, custom paintwork, and he even developed a sideline doing Morris Minor conversion kits as Kelly Products.

Moving to Brisbane in the early 90s, Paul gave cars a rest for a spell and did coachbuilding and design work on buses, but was drawn back in to create his legendary Smooth Customs shop. Sometimes working with an offsider and sometimes solo, Paul has amassed an incredible portfolio of high-end rods and customs, and contributed specialised parts to countless more.

All the while, he's remained a steadfast evangelist for custom cars and their local heritage. He took his gas axe to the first-ever *Street Machine* project car – Geoff Paradise's long-suffering '57 – and has worked tirelessly to preserve the history of Aussie customs with his camera while pushing the case for customising through articles in other mags like *Street & Custom*, *Super Street* and *The Newsledder*. He remains a valued advisor to the current *SM* editorial team.

STORY SIMON TELFORD **PHOTOS** *SM* ARCHIVES

ABOVE: Bluey Boxsell's Windsor-powered VW Beetle is an icon of the Sydney scene and first appeared in *SM*, Dec '83-'Jan '84. In 1990, Paul treated it to a killer roof chop

RIGHT: Paul worked on the restoration of 'Captain' Bob Hamilton's hot-rodded '57 DeSoto Fireflite, including some of the bodywork, the right-hand drive conversion, and creating a stack of clever custom parts to make it complete

'57 DeSoto Fireflite

BELOW: Paul McKennariey's internationally renowned '48 Hudson sled (*SM*, Jul '05) is one of the crowning achievements of Paul's career

BOB KOTMEL

THROUGH the pages of *Street Machine* and other mags, Bob Kotmel taught a couple of generations how to go drag racing. His magazine columns were aspirational but firmly no-bullshit, and always based on verifiable, repeatable results.

Bob taught us not only how to build engines and set up suspensions, but how to save money when going racing. Common sense was his forte. From him we learned that you don't race dynos and to instead trust in the Moroso calculator.

Bob put his money where his mouth was and tested his theories on his own cars, but always with the counsel of a brains trust of racers and engine builders from across the country. Through him, talented folk such as Peter Michaels, Steve Gay, Phil Soderstrom, Sam and Izzy Blumenstein and many more transmitted their knowledge into the minds of countless impressionable youngsters.

Given that he grew up in his grandfather's engine shop in Melbourne, Bob was born for the job. "My toys were presses, lathes and drills," he reckons.

He moved to Mackay, Queensland in 1971 to work as a fitter and turner, but fast cars, kick-start Harleys, surfing and rock 'n' roll would be his passions.

His signature vehicle was his HG Holden ute, affectionately known as Old Sludge. The HG was a rolling test bed for countless Holden V8 combinations that provided much of the content for his columns for years. By the time Bob finally sold the ute, it would have had almost 2000 passes under its belt.

Bob was first asked to pen a technical story by Geoff Paradise in 1978, for *Van Wheels*. Soon after *Van Wheels* transformed into *Street Machine*, Paro invited Bob to be its new tech editor. When Paro split to start up *Performance Street Car* in 1985, Bob followed, but returned to the fold in June '92 with his Stage Write column, which he continued until 2020.

These days Bob gets his kicks riding the wheels off his Panhead chopper, playing the heck out of his Fender Strat, and continuing to advocate for go-fast innovation.

STORY SIMON TELFORD **PHOTOS** SIMON DAVIDSON & *SM* ARCHIVES

ABOVE & INSERT: In 1989, Bob went to the US and crewed for Bill Kuhlmann's Chev Beretta, the world's quickest Doorslammer at the time. "It won 11 meetings in a row," says Bob. He also crewed for Robbie Vandergriff's Soft Seal 1957 Chev, which Bob still rates as one of the all-time great race cars

RIGHT: Of all the streeters he has owned, Bob's favourite is an HQ van with Stonehenge and moonscape murals applied by Joe Pace. A hot small-block Chev powered the pano to low 13s through the mufflers on street tyres. Sadly, it got written off by three cows on a low-flying run back from Surfers in 1983

Bill Kuhlmann and Bob

HQ panel van

Old Sludge HG ute

Seddo, Bob and Paro

PALMYRA DRAG CLUB

SAMS AUTO REPAIRS

"Lawman"

386

Bob's first race car of note was a big-block '57 Chev Super Stocker dubbed Lawman, which was the quickest A/MP Super Stocker in the land for the time, though it couldn't quite match Rob Madden's record of 11.5 seconds in his '55

93

T-6 Texan pilot

NORM LONGFIELD

NORM Longfield was a teenager when he caught the now-legendary Australian Drag Fest Tour at Castlereagh Dragway in 1966. "I fell in love right then and there," says Norm. "The Yanks were running high-sevens in their dragsters. It took me 40 years to get one of my own."

Norm's first race car was typical for a kid in the mid-60s – an FJ Holden with a hot grey motor, rollpans, metallic paint and Kustom City mags. "My dad was a mechanic, taught me everything," he says. "Dad wouldn't actually do anything, but he'd stand there all day. He said if he did it for me, I wouldn't learn. But he never understood why we'd go street racing on Saturday night, break it, then work on it all day Sunday to drive to work on Monday."

When the FJ got defected for running 12-inch wheels, Norm decided to build a T-bucket. "The only cars the cops had no specifications on were hot rods," he recalls. "They didn't know much about them. I'm going back to 1968. There were no such things as engineering reports; you just took it over the pits. It wasn't hard to get them registered.

"We took it to Castlereagh, and down the deep end is when you realise you're just sitting on a chassis! No rollcage, just bits of timber and fibreglass and upholstery. You're bulletproof when you're 20."

Norm was conscripted shortly afterwards and served in Vietnam. "I'd never been out of New South Wales, so it was like a big adventure," he says. "One time we took off to Saigon, just drove out the gate. We were 100km from base camp for three days, three of us, going up all these back roads. If we'd got ambushed, no one would have had a clue. It was like racing a T-bucket with no rollbar."

TOP RIGHT: "It's a hot rod with wings, a real handful," says Norm of his 1943 North American Aviation T-6 Texan warbird, powered by a supercharged 1340ci nine-cylinder radial engine. "You have to have all the respect in the world for it or it will bite, like a hot rod. It's a beautiful thing to fly"

Norm's shed

Rhonda and Norm

When he returned in one piece, Norm set about working for himself, married his wife Rhonda, and they bought a house. Once he was up and running, he got back into cars, starting with the blown Corvette that can be seen on the cover of the first-ever *Street Machine & Van Wheels*, October-November 1981.

From there, Norm's builds became increasingly more ambitious and creative, starting with a rear-engined Model A pick-up with an 8/71-blown and injected big-block running on methanol. It looked unlike any other car on earth, and the best part was it was registered as a Ford stump-puller tractor.

Next was a Willys masterpiece built on a full chassis and running a nitro-burning blown Milodon Hemi and Lenco trans. It was built to be driven, shown and raced.

After that came a Jocko Liner, an experimental, temperamental and beautiful American drag car designed by Robert 'Jocko' Johnson in the 50s. "When I saw it advertised for sale, I couldn't pass it up," says Norm. "At that stage I didn't know much about them, didn't know how many were around, but I could tell it was a really rare car."

Norm and Ziggy Sadler treated the car to a concours-level restoration, but that didn't stop Norm from racing it. He eventually pranged it while racing against an aeroplane (yep) at Cowra Airport, and the car copped another, even better resto for a new life as a cackle car.

Never fear, these days Norm still has plenty of ways to slake his need for speed, including a nitro front-engined dragster and a 1943 North American Aviation T-6 Texan aircraft.

STORY GEOFF SEDDON **PHOTOS** PETER BATEMAN & *SM* ARCHIVES

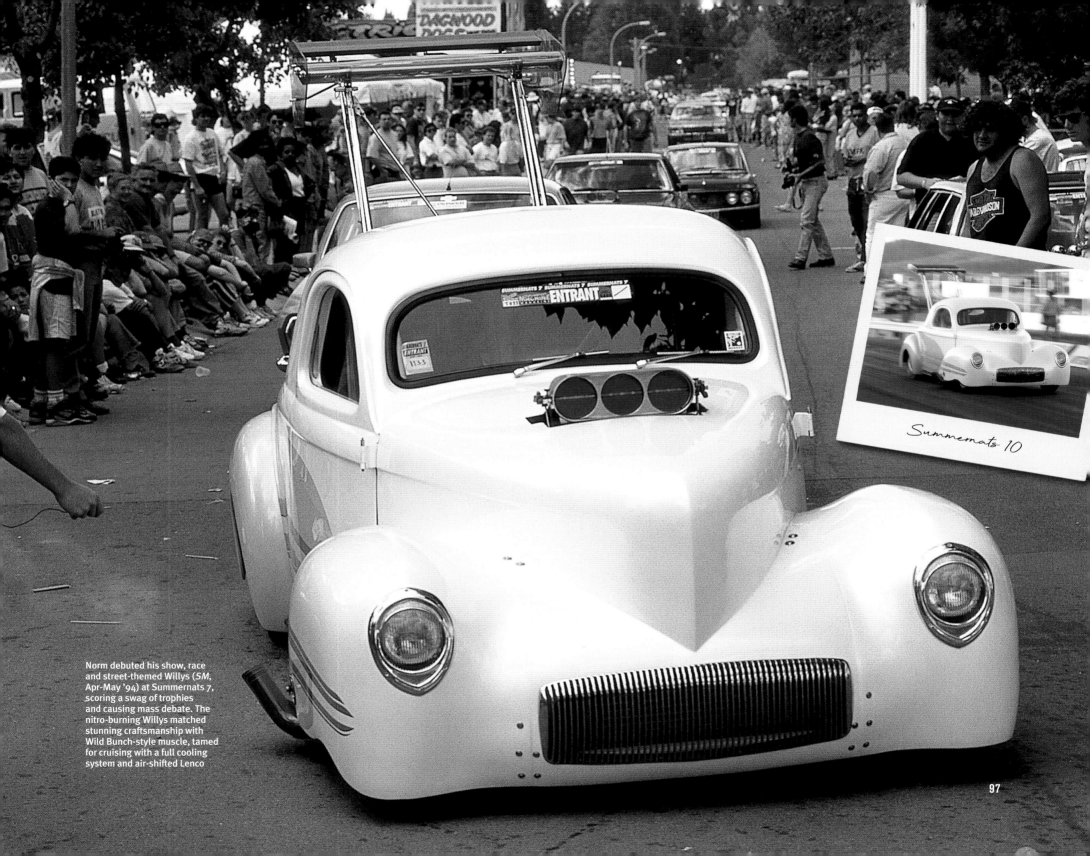

Summernats 10

Norm debuted his show, race and street-themed Willys (*SM*, Apr-May '94) at Summernats 7, scoring a swag of trophies and causing mass debate. The nitro-burning Willys matched stunning craftsmanship with Wild Bunch-style muscle, tamed for cruising with a full cooling system and air-shifted Lenco

Lake Gairdner 2001

Summernats 8

Initially tunnel-rammed, GM176 (*SM*, Jun '89) went blown in time for the first Summernats in 1988 and went on to win three Burnout Championships in a row from 'Nats 6 to 8. The king had arrived!

SMOTY 2001

GM·176

GARY MYERS

AT THE *Street Machine* Respect Awards held in 2011 to celebrate the 30th anniversary of the mag, then-editor Geoff Seddon presented the Mr Street Machine award to Gary Myers. "We looked for an individual who encompassed what we were all about," said Seddo. "Someone whose example stands for so much of what we are and what we do."

From Narrandera, NSW, Gary Myers has dedicated a large portion of his time on earth to building, racing, cruising, and, of course, skidding cars. John Peterson invented the modern-day burnout, but Gary took it to the masses.

Gary made his name with a black '66 Mustang wearing the number plates GM176 – a car he's owned since he was 18. He campaigned the car at the Street Machine Nationals in 1984 and '86 with a tunnel-rammed Windsor, before going blown for Summernats 1. Its first *SM* feature appeared in the June '89 issue.

The Mustang quickly became a dominant force, with Gary winning three Summernats Burnout Championships on the trot from 1993 to '95, as well as several Go-to-Whoa wins, the Burnout Championship of the World in 2000, and two Burnout Masters crowns.

GM176 got a significant birthday at the turn of the millennium, which saw Gary rewarded with his first Street Machine of the Year win in 2001. That same year he took the car to Lake Gairdner and ran 170mph – an impressive effort from a basic 302 Windsor.

The salt trip was something out of left field, and an indicator that Gary and his wife Deby wanted to branch out from burnouts into other areas. Another of those areas was event promotion, starting with the inaugural Gazzanats in 2004. This was the first big event run by competitors and it paved the way for many of the great competitor-run events we have today.

By that time, Gary was deep into the build of another '66 Mustang, with the lofty aim of creating an elite car the likes of which had never been seen in Australia. Like Rod Hadfield, Gary tends to plan his builds years or even decades ahead, slowly gathering parts, information and inspiration.

That second Mustang was the Silver Bullet, which, from top to bottom, was super-smooth and featured a ton of body mods, including a roof chop to further accentuate the height of the twin-supercharged 392 Hemi sticking out of what was left of the bonnet. It was a massive hit, winning the MotorEx Superstars award, Summernats Grand Champion and SMOTY in 2005.

The Myers clan

While Gary is now synonymous with Mustangs, his big love is actually XA Falcons, which led to his next major project, the Repco XACUTER, built from a written-off GT coupe.

"The idea with XACUTER was to show that we could win the Summernats Burnout Championship with an aspirated car," says Gary. "It was a quick build once we started, and it debuted at Summernats in 2008. It never quite got there, so we parked it after a couple of years."

After that came 2INSANE, a 2005 Mustang with a blown and injected small-block built with the guidance of West Australian racer and tuner George Separovich. It was built to run big numbers on the salt, but various commitments – including an expanded Gazzanats series – kept Gary away from Lake Gairdner. The car subsequently saw some action as a burnout and powerskid car.

In 2014, Gary handed GM176 down to his son Jake, who reimagined it as S1CKO. Jake took to skids like he was born to do it and has gone on to win the Burnout Masters twice, at Summernats 32 and 35.

All the while, Gary was planning to revamp XACUTER, funnelling his newfound knowledge into his ultimate blown and injected small-block Ford. He couldn't have been more successful, bringing the car's visuals right up to date and completely transforming its performance. The car, re-dubbed AGROXA, went on to win the 2017 Street Machine of the Year vote by a wide margin.

At the time of writing, the S1CKO Mustang has had yet another makeover, this time back to its all-black 80s look. And with Jake soon to debut a fresh burnout car of his own, the plan is to eventually put both GM176 and AGROXA back to street duties. Watch out for them cruising at a rod run near you!

TOP LEFT: The Silver Bullet '66 Mustang (*SM*, Sep '04) originally ran 8/71 and 6/71 blowers stacked with four-pot Hilborn injection. Gary then went to a single blower and Enderle hat set-up, before reverting to the twin-blown set-up and selling the car, which now lives in the US

MIDDLE LEFT: The 2INSANE '05 Mustang (*SM*, Dec '12) was built with Lake Gairdner in mind, but while that hasn't happened, the car has proved to be an able performer in both burnouts and powerskids

BOTTOM LEFT: The first iteration of Gary's XA was the naturally aspirated XACUTER. A name change to AGROXA and a blown revamp (*SM*, Aug '17) saw it take out a third SMOTY for Gary and Deby in 2017

STORY SIMON TELFORD **PHOTOS** *SM* ARCHIVES

The GM176 Mustang has run under the name S1CKO with son Jake behind the wheel for the past decade. But for Summernats 35, Gary and Jake gave the car a makeover that harked back to its appearance at 'Nats 1, complete with five-slotter rims and the Mustang's original wheelie bars

GM·176
THE KING

A Crower-injected big-block Chev took centre stage for Wayne's tidy HJ ute (*SM*, Jun '88), which was built in a three-week thrash for Summernats. It was initially a stop-gap car while his XF Falcon pro streeter was in the build. "The plan was to refit that engine back into the XF, but that project was dragging on and eventually I lost interest and sold it off"

RAT

WAYNE PAGEL

A FOUNDING father of Australia's pro street movement, Wayne Pagel shook the foundations of our sport with a legendary HT Monaro that we featured in the June 1986 issue. Although officially dubbed Midnight Maniac, it has become universally known by what was on its number plates: GAS69.

"I was a product of the panel van era, and at 18, I kicked off with an HG van that was a dead-stocker six-cylinder," Wayne says. "I got interested in the horsepower side of cars. I fitted a 350 Chev and tinkered with it inside and out."

Wayne bought a show-quality black HT Monaro from Rob Beauchamp as a roller for $3500. It was repainted black with candy blue for the engine bay before he slotted in his 350 Chev and headed to the 1985 Street Machine Nationals.

"The problem was, people just walked straight past it, which can be tough to swallow when it's your pride and joy," says Wayne. "I made an instant decision to make it tough and mean for the following year.

"The pro street style was in its infancy, and it was the ultimate style as far as I was concerned. I wanted a low and fat Monaro. It had Weld wheels and imported Enderle injection. A fabricator by the name of Scott Leo, along with a band of mates, helped get it done, and it won Entrants' Choice and Top Street Comp in 1986."

A plethora of high-quality rides have been built in the Pagel shed in the decades since. "I was involved in the builds of Bill Murfin's Billet Monaro and Al 'Bundy' Lucas's SMOTY-winning HQ, so I kept my toes in the water with those cars, and also with the Queensland division of the Australian Street Machine Federation," explains Wayne.

Nowadays, Wayne, his wife Sandy and his son Reece all have stand-out rides to their credit. "Sandy has been instrumental in getting our cars finished over the past 35 years," Wayne says. "Reece has grown up with cars, so he has a solid grounding in what is involved to finish a project. I couldn't be prouder of the pair of them."

STORY SIMON MAJOR **PHOTOS** *SM* ARCHIVES

ABOVE & RIGHT: "For many years, I thought GAS69 was just my memory," Wayne says. "Social media opened up a whole world of people who still remember it so fondly after so long; I had no idea it inspired people the way it did." What wasn't to love, with its fat and low stance, deep black paint, blown and injected small-block and big 'n' little Weld wheels? The fact that GAS69 is still highly revered years later is vindication of Wayne's vision and innovation

BOTTOM RIGHT: Wayne's XY ute was meant to be a tidy tow rig to haul around his other HT Monaro drag car but ended up a beautifully detailed magazine cover car

Performance **STREET CAR**

OCT./NOV. 1993

$5.00*
NZ $6.60

YOKOHAMA *Performance Car* SHOOTOUT
Details inside....

OFF-STREET DRAGS

Cylinder Head Flow Facts
Dyno Tuning
EFI Basics

PAGEL'S PURPLE PICK-UP

Young Paro in '75

A dream backyard for a street machiner in the 1970s – and now!

104

Paro with Dave Cook

VK SS road test

Paro with Hemi

GEOFF PARADISE 1954-2015

STREET *Machine* founder Geoff Paradise got his start in the mag biz in 1970 when, as a 16-year-old apprentice spray painter, he wrote to Kevin Wolfe, the editor of *Australian Hot Rodding Review*, to complain about the quality of the pictures. Wolfe wrote back: "If you think you can do better, do it yourself." Geoff promptly did just that and was paid $16 for his first feature. Within three years he was the editor of the magazine.

Geoff then moved to the US and picked up a job as features editor on the world's biggest-selling car magazine, *Hot Rod*. Here, his entrepreneurial streak was on display, replacing the mag's expensive and time-consuming colour separation process with a cheaper and faster system using his contacts from his time on *AHRR*. Immigration hassles forced his return to Australia in 1976.

By this time, *AHRR* had floundered and was replaced by *Van Wheels*. Armed with what he had learned, Paradise tried to convince Murray Publishing to let him start a new mag in the style of *Hot Rod*'s sister publication, *Car Craft*. The suits said no, so he edited the drag racing newspaper *Drag News* for a while, and later did stints as a reporter for the ABC and AAP.

By 1980, the van craze was losing momentum. And so was *Van Wheels* magazine, which had been badly neglected by management. Geoff was invited to take over the reins and, with the support of managing editor Mac Douglas, was finally able to create his Aussie version of *Car Craft*. In issue 10, he announced: "In future issues of *Van Wheels*, you are going to see vans so customised they will resemble sedans, sedans with blowers, sedans with turbochargers, sedans with fat tyres. I fink *[sic]* they call them street machines."

Paro and Plankkman

ABOVE: One of Geoff's greatest coups was the V8 'Til '98 campaign, which helped extend the life of the Holden V8 far longer than anyone could have hoped for

TOP LEFT: The *SM* crew circa 1983 (L-R): art director Lindsay Hannington, journo John Wright, Geoff, artist John Taylor, ad dudes Stephen Miller and John Miller, and production guy Swanee

ABOVE: Paro and *SM* columnist Brian Plankkman check out the Holden red motor production line. Plankkman's close friend Phil Scott would get the editor's gig when Paradise left to start *Performance Street Car*

And so, in 1981, *Van Wheels & Street Machine* was released, with John Strachan's Alley Cat and Dave Ryan's GTO on the cover. For the next issue, the title was altered to *Street Machine & Van Wheels*, with the *Van Wheels* reference dropping off by issue six. By this time, *Street Machine* was selling 30,000 copies a month, a figure Geoff took to 55,000 when he put Chris Christou's tyre-smoking Phase III on the August-September 1984 cover, beating stablemate *Wheels* for the first time.

He fell out with management shortly after and founded *Performance Street Car* and then later *Fast Fours & Rotaries*, *Australian Drag Racer*, *Hot 4s* and more. He went on to publish *Transport & Trucking Today* and *Coach & Bus*, and in more recent times worked in a PR role at Mercedes-Benz.

All the while, Paro remained a passionate enthusiast, finishing his famous '57 Heaven project in 2006 and even building a blown Hemi-powered '32 roadster. He was a genuine car and bike guy to his bones. As a publisher, he was a true innovator, as well a mentor and a mate to many in the industry, young and old.

STORY GEOFF SEDDON **PHOTOS** PETER BATEMAN & *SM* ARCHIVES

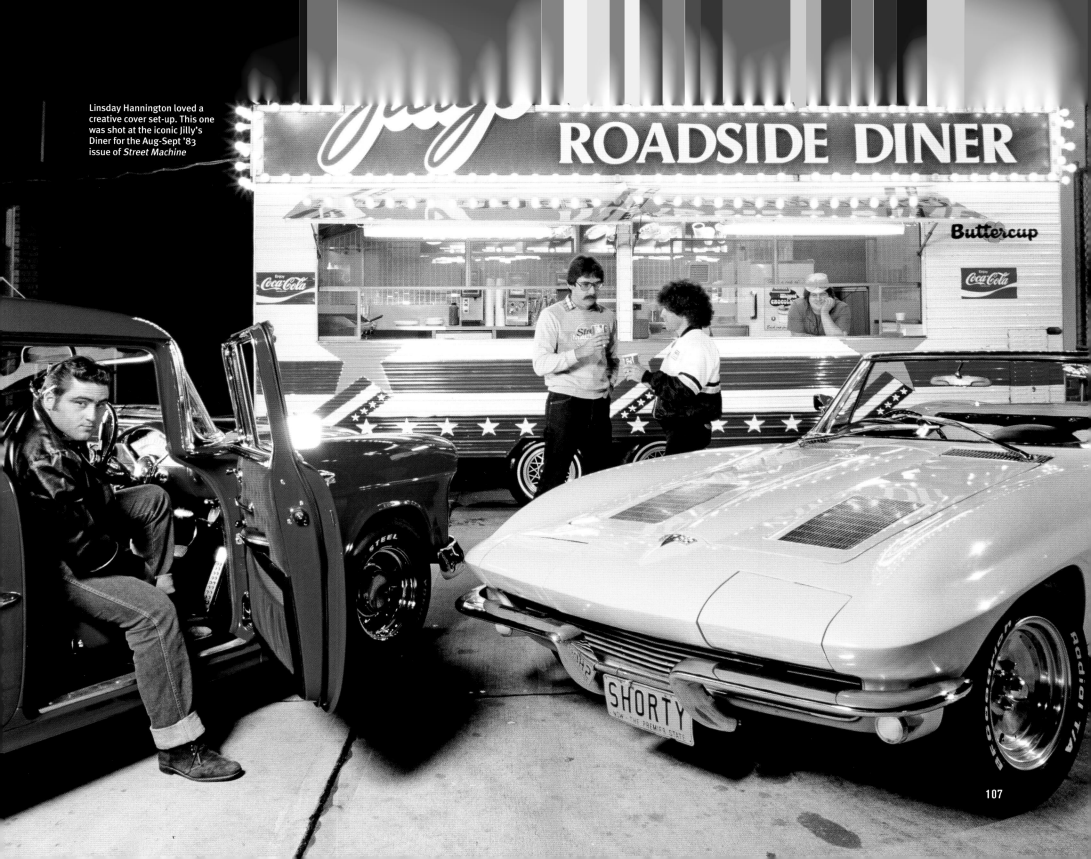

Linsday Hannington loved a creative cover set-up. This one was shot at the iconic Jilly's Diner for the Aug-Sept '83 issue of *Street Machine*

ROADSIDE DINER

SMOTY 1991

Baby Cup HQ

TUFF·XY

NSW

Thunderdome, '91

CRAIG PARKER

STREET Machine editor Geoff Seddon (who reigned from 2000 to 2013) clearly recalls when Craig Parker's job application lobbed on his desk in 2001. "I remember his CV – there's his name, his address and his achievements: Winner of Street Machine of the Year 1991. I thought, 'F–k, I need this guy.' I wanted that genius on the team, that car genius."

We're not sure if Craig thought his TUFFXY would be his ticket to a job at *SM*, but his SMOTY win in '91 certainly brought him fame and a $10,000 fortune. He started the project as a first-year apprentice, and three years, four girlfriends and 50 grand later, he had built a car that remains iconic to this day. How Craig put in the hours on the XY while working multiple jobs to pay for it all, we'll never know.

The XY was influenced by Group C touring cars and as such had a real road racer vibe, with radically altered suspension and pumped guards. Its killer wheel and tyre package mated three-piece alloy Dragways to Neale Wheels centres, wrapped in fat Pirelli rubber.

Craig showed the car extensively, travelling all over the country, including a trip to the Street Machine Nationals at Calder Park, where it won Top Overall Street Machine and People's Choice, and topped 200 clicks around the Calder Park Thunderdome.

His next build was a Summernats cruiser, dubbed Baby Cup, with mates John Hatton and Bill Westwood. The boys punched out the roofless wonder in just three months for the grand total of $1500! The HQ was dropped on its guts, channelled and treated to extended sills for maximum lowness. It was a star of Summernats 6 and was sold before the event even finished.

Once ensconced in the features editor chair at *Street Machine*, Craig project-managed two of our most famed giveaway cars – VUFORU and the Comfort Cruiser Galaxie.

STORY SIMON TELFORD **PHOTOS** PETER BATEMAN & *SM* ARCHIVES

ABOVE: Craig describes the Comfort Cruiser '67 Galaxie project as a "manic makeover". Highlights included the HOK Candy Apple Red respray, stark white custom trim by Rides By Kam, Carson-style roof by Cliff Carter and 18- and 20-inch Intro rims. The pièce de résistance was the custom billet grille created by all-round genius Paul Librio

RIGHT: With the XY long gone, Craig these days has a veritable fleet of toughies at home to choose from: a '32 Ford roadster, a '67 US Fairlane hardtop, a '66 Nova and a 427-cube Shafiroff-powered XF ute

BELOW & FAR RIGHT: VUFORU was a big project. Fitting the then-huge 22-inch rims called for mini-tubs, lengthened wheelarches and serious mods to the IRS bum, thanks to Waddington Street Rods. Hi-Tech Rods fabbed the billet grille, and Precise Trim turned the interior into a sea of bright red. The wild paint scheme was designed by Ryan Carter and applied by Mat Egan and Earl Webber

Craig's collection

VUFORU

GEOFF PATON

WHEN all-round car guy Geoff Paton decided to combine work with pleasure by purchasing Super Plus Speed Shop in Dandenong, Victoria in 1979, the idea of hitting a drag strip in anger had not yet crossed his mind. He'd never have predicted that within a few short years he'd become an icon of the early pro streeting movement and enjoy fame behind the wheel of some of the most spectacular, well-engineered and popular cars of the era.

Frequent business trips to the US throughout the 80s saw Geoff count Keith Black, the Summers brothers, Pete Jackson and the guys at Carrillo as friends, but Geoff's inspiration to go racing came from those around him. Most of his staff and customers were racing cars, so why not him?

A white LX Torana hatch kicked things off, running a 12.78 under Chev power and giving Geoff a taste for more. Several other builds followed, although his spectacular, wheelstanding Mk1 Cortina is perhaps his most fondly remembered.

Having a mechanical engineering degree helped Geoff hone his craft, as did his early career working at Mercedes-Benz's R&D division in Stuttgart. His focus on adapting factory suspension systems to both work on the street and launch at the track helped propel him to guru status among pro street fanatics.

Geoff's greatest racing success came in 1989 when he took out the premier street car class at the inaugural Australian Street Machine Drag Racing Championships at Calder Park driving a big block-powered HJ Holden. He'd sold Super Plus not long before entering the event and quickly found out that racing was a lot harder without cheap parts, workshop space and free labour!

Some people enjoy a lifelong career in a particular industry and wind up becoming legends through sheer longevity, while others like Geoff build a legacy in just a few short years and then walk off into the sunset. "I still like tinkering on cars, but I ended up going in a completely different direction," he says. "I certainly made a lot of friends and had a lot of fun along the way – loved every minute!"

STORY DAVE CAREY **PHOTOS** SM ARCHIVES

ABOVE: Geoff's gassed King Rat A9X Torana featured on the cover of *SM* in August-September '85. While it wasn't the first 9sec street car in Oz, the story and cover ignited an arms race that continues to this day!

LEFT: The nitrous-sucking, big-block Chev-powered Mk1 Cortina held the national SS/A Super Sedan record in 1987 with a 9.52sec ET, and eventually ran a best time of 9.36

OPPOSITE PAGE: The Australian Street Machine Drag Racing Championships in 1989 was an early ancestor of Drag Challenge. Geoff won that meeting driving Robin Waite's HJ, re-powered by an alloy 482ci big-block imported from the US. The motor made 726hp and the HJ ran a best of 10.18@132mph

Chev-powered MK1 Cortina

Geoff's EH

Calder Park, '89

The concept of the burnout as competitive performance art was born at Heathcote in 1977. JP joined in what passed for a burnout comp in those days and eclipsed any other attempts by powerskidding the length of the quarter, turning around and repeating the feat all the way back to the startline, before popping the tyres and driving off on the rims

JOHN PETERSON 1946-2019

THEY say you should never meet your heroes, but I've never heard of anyone who was disappointed after coming in contact with John Peterson. JP was one of the founding fathers of the street machine movement and a folk hero to Ford fans everywhere.

The extent of his influence on our sport is unfathomable. Before JP, a burnout was a short skid that proper drag racers did to warm up their tyres. But John turned burnouts into an artform for street cars.

While JP and his black Mk3 Zephyr are most famous for their burnouts, the pair also scored big on the show circuit and made a wicked combination on the strip. All the while, the Zephyr, or Dark Horse, was driven to events with John's family on board. He loved the idea that a street car could also be a race car and a show car.

The Zephyr's underdog status was a factor in the Peterson mystique, its humble 289 Windsor punching well above its weight. John's enthusiasm for the Blue Oval – and vocal hatred of anything with a GM badge! – further solidified his appeal among a certain section of the audience.

JP sold the Dark Horse in the late 80s and built a white version, which appeared at the seventh Nationals in 1987. This was fitted with a stove-hot 302, Doug Nash five-speed, three-quarter chassis and tubs.

"John had some issues with his back and dropped out of the car scene for a while after that," says his wife Margaret. "But when he started working with Norm and Vicki at Aussie Desert Cooler, he found his love for the scene again."

John passed away in 2019, prompting outpourings of grief from around the country. The most public tribute came at Summernats 33, where Peter Gray's Camaro was decked out with JP289 plates and its tyres were packed with John's ashes. After a minute's silence before the Burnout Masters final, Peter delivered a blue-tinged smoke show to make the old master proud.

And at Summernats 35, the John Peterson Burnout Hall of Fame was established in his honour, with JP its first inductee.

STORY SIMON TELFORD **PHOTOS** SIMON DAVIDSON & *SM* ARCHIVES

RIGHT: JP got a hero's welcome when he returned to Canberra after many years to skid at Summernats 21 in 2008

BELOW: At the fourth Street Machine Nationals in 1980, John won both the burnout competition and the Go-to-Whoa, establishing himself as the burnout king. This was followed by the first and last burnout show ever staged on the streets of Melbourne's CBD for the 1982 Moomba Festival!

Moomba '82

Summernats 21

Norm Longfield's Willys

GREG 'ZIGGY' SADLER

GREG 'Ziggy' Sadler grew up riding his pushbike to panel van shows and ended up becoming one of Australia's top car builders, a show judge both here and in the US, and much more.

"I don't know how I got into cars," says Ziggy. "Nobody in my family was into them. But I started taking myself to panel van and hot rod shows like Roselands from a very young age. My mum didn't know, but I'd ride my bike for miles to get to shows or catch the train. I didn't have any money for admission, so I'd sneak in during set-up time. I met guys like Pat Fay, Chris Cummings and Rob Howard and would pepper them with questions. Eventually, Chris Cummings said, 'If you're going to annoy me, you may as well learn to polish!' I was hooked from then on."

Ziggy finished school in 1979 and the following Monday started an apprenticeship panel beating and later spray painting at a car dealer. From there, he cut his teeth at various restoration shops, including gigs working on high-end stuff like Rolls-Royces and Porsches.

Ziggy's P-plate car was a channelled '32 roadster, but he found the rod scene unwelcoming and instead found a home with the Street Machine Association. He began working with Graham Stubbs as a show judge when he was still in his early 20s. This led to Ziggy judging at the first *Street Machine* Summernats, and later on he judged for Mothers at the SEMA Show.

For a decade or so, he did training and testing for paint companies like Wattyl, Dulux and DuPont, while on the side he worked his body and paint magic on some now-iconic cars, most notably two of Norm Longfield's weapons – the pro street Willys (*SM*, Apr-May '94) and the restored Jocko Liner salt racer (*SM*, Feb '13).

Ziggy's Hot Rods was born in the late 90s, with Mike Kluver's '68 Mustang (*SM*, Nov '10), dubbed Warhorse 427, being just one of its standout builds. The shop is now renamed Ziggy's Design Driven to better reflect its mission, and Ziggy and his team continue to push the envelope with several long-term, concept car-style builds, including a VW Karmann Ghia named Karmageddon.

STORY GLENN TORRENS **PHOTOS** PETER BATEMAN & *SM* ARCHIVES

ABOVE: Ziggy helped revive Norm Longfield's Jocko Liner twice – once when it first lobbed Down Under looking like a worn-out surfboard, and again after the car crashed while racing a warplane on an airstrip

LEFT: Ziggy manufactured these killer billet trophies for the first 10 years of Meguiar's MotorEx

Project Karmageddon

Mike Kluver's '68 Mustang won the first-ever Street Elite Showcase at MotorEx 2010, scoring firsts in Design/Execution, Engine Bay and Engineering

Summernats 8

Heatseeker HK

Howard Astill's *ROCK 3*

Working on *ROCK 3*

MARK SANDERS

PRO touring is all about horsepower coupled with world-class handling, something Mark Sanders has been building into his cars since before the term pro touring was coined. He pre-empted it all way back in '91 when he re-debuted his 4.4-litre alloy V8-swapped LH Torana following a comprehensive rebuild, and was featured in the April-May issue of *Street Machine* that year.

The P76-powered Torry sat lower and turned harder than any Torana had a right to, thanks to custom-created double A-arm front suspension inspired by Mark's love of touring car racing. We didn't have to wait long for a follow-up, with Mark's less-is-more HK Monaro appearing in the October-November 1994 issue of *Street Machine*. Back then, he described the Monaro's theme as an evolution: "Inside, it's a full restoration. Outside, it's a lightly modified restoration. Under the bonnet, it's a contemporary street machine. And underneath, it's a full-on hot rod. There's a transition from one area to another."

The Monaro's massive chassis and suspension mods not only cradled a big-block Chev and heavy-duty top loader four-speed, but rendered it fully street legal in South Australia at a time when a lot of modified cars flouted the law.

Mark's aim for the Monaro was two-fold. Aside from challenging the status quo, it also served to promote his chassis fabrication business, Road Performance Modifications. Of his many customers, Neville Phillips remains among the most famous, or more so, Neville's Sanders-fettled EH Holden, LEGAL8.

117

STREET MACHINE MARCH '91
$4.50
NZ$6.95 (INCL GST)

TWO CHANCES TO WIN... COMPLETE SUSPENSION GEAR!

MONSTER 32 PAGE SUMMERNATS REPORT
+ COOL CRUISIN' + BIG BURNOUTS

THE A TEAM!

AUSTRALIA'S NEW BREED OF RADICAL STREET CARS

LEFT: We featured Mark's P76-powered Torana in the December '90 issue. Painted white, Mark got it built and legal for just $12,000. He gave it a big makeover and it scored the cover of the March '91 mag. Now painted blue, the LH had copped a full chassis, fabricated front suspension, UC dash, hidden wiper motor, and a race-style pedal box. It picked up Top Pro Street, Top Pro Street Engineered and a Top 10 trophy at Summernats 4

BELOW: Under LEGAL8's fibreglass bonnet is a tough 308, stirred by a top loader four-speed and a Ford 9in with a three-link rear end, Spax coil-overs and mini-tubs, resulting in a fully legal pro touring monster. Owner Neville Phillips has attacked Summernats, Targa Tasmania, the Dutton Rally, Targa Adelaide, regularity sprints and the Aussie Muscle Car Run since, racking up over 40,000 hard miles

OPPOSITE PAGE: One of Mark's current projects is this 1969 250SL Merc. He's building it as a cruiser, with the factory running gear turfed in favour of a 308 and TH350 deal, an HG front end with a Commodore rack, and three- or four-link rear suspension with a Watt's link

Mark Sanders

LEGAL8, featured in the July-August 1992 issue of *SM*, not only purported to be SA's first fully legal V8-powered early Holden, but it had the ability to stop, go and turn like few before it.

A chance meeting with Howard Astill at the Street Machine Nationals resulted in Mark collaborating with Howard on the iconic ROCK 3 XA Falcon. "I was young and brash, and started telling him his car was shit, with ladder bars and the like," Mark says. "Fortunately, he listened and challenged me to do better."

Howard allowed Mark to attack ROCK SOLID 2 with an angle grinder in order to create a show-stopping Ford that handled just as well as his Holdens. They later worked together on the ROCK 4 Compact Fairlane and Howard's SMOTY-winning RACE ROCK XA hardtop.

When you look at Mark's body of work, his list of influences make perfect sense. "Ian Hazel lived a block away, and his PREM70 HG wagon left a lasting impression – so subtle, yet so detailed, so well finished," Mark says. "A lot of the Monaro was inspired by PREM70.

"Later, I met Colin Townsend [of 1994 SMOTY-winning FJ fame] when I concreted his garage. He taught me a lot. He's a clever man who had a lot to do with the original Torana build and me starting my business, RPM."

For Mark, professional satisfaction had been all about the engineering – how a car worked rather than how it looked.

"Howard Astill and Ron Barclay changed that," he says. "Howard led me down the path of show cars, trophies, marketing and sponsorship. Ron was the guy that really taught me detail."

Mark remains a legend in the street machining community, not only for his technically wondrous builds that predicted the emergence of pro touring, but for their timelessness. Rest assured, he's still creating, now working on a V6-powered full-chassis '68 Karmann Ghia and a 308-powered '69 Mercedes 250SL.

STORY DAVE CAREY **PHOTOS** TROY BARKER & *SM* ARCHIVES

'69 Merc project

Seddo's HK Monaro

Seddo hits the pad with Victor
Bray at Springnats 2003

120

Seddo's Galaxie

GEOFF SEDDON

WHEN Geoff 'Seddo' Seddon became editor of *Street Machine* in 2000, the magazine was almost 20 years old. It was still a great thing, but was in need of a reboot.

The mag was only coming out nine times a year and sales weren't what they could have been. With Seddo at the helm, *SM* got a serious injection of investment, enthusiasm and talent, driving sales through the roof and setting a template that we still follow today.

While he'd been a car guy since birth, it was actually his passion for motorcycles that got Seddo into the magazine scene, first with contributions to *Ozbike*, then later road testing for *Two Wheels*. Ditching a shiny-bum gig with Tooheys Brewery, Seddo steered into magazine work full-time in 1988 before graduating to editor of *Performance Street Bike* in 1990.

A short stint as founding editor of *Ralph* magazine – where the suits had way too much to say – steeled him to ensure such a terrible corporate fate would not befall his next baby, *Street Machine*.

"Management's view of *Street Machine* when I arrived was, 'Oh, they're all bogans,'" Seddo says. "'Knuckle-draggers' was the word they used to use for our readers. I hated that shit. I had a mullet, wore flannelette shirts and liked old Holdens. So that was a real motivation for when I got there, to change that perception, and to get a bit more respect for it within the company and outside, too."

With support from publisher Brad Boxall, Seddo set about rebuilding *SM* from the ground up. The publishing schedule went from nine issues per year to 12, he hired gun writers like Curt Dupriez and SMOTY winner Craig Parker, and installed a stellar art team.

Content-wise, Seddo embraced the outlaw side of our culture while honouring the sport's elders, broke some dumb and antiquated rules about publishing (no American cars on the front cover!), and injected a good dose of humour and lifestyle.

His formula worked. Sales and advertising exploded and awards followed, including Magazine of the Year and Editor of the Year, and Seddo was bestowed with a Rare Spares Legends golden helmet at Summernats 26 in 2013.

STORY SIMON TELFORD **PHOTOS** *SM* ARCHIVES

ABOVE: "My favourite cover is the September 2001 issue starring Simon Kryger's INOCNT Torana," says Seddo. "That really captured what we were trying to do"

LEFT: Geoff was stunned when he was awarded Rare Spares Legend status at Summernats 26, joining the likes of Rod Hadfield and Howard Astill

GRAHAM STUBBS 1945-2013

FROM the mid-60s through to the early 70s, Graham Stubbs could be found at Castlereagh International Dragway campaigning his street-driven, six-banger '55 with clocklike regularity.

That '55 was never a headline act, but Graham was doing what he loved. To him, the challenge was getting the best out of the stovebolt and cutting a good light. My history books don't go back far enough to establish whether Graham ever had a big win. To him, that didn't matter. It was all about the thrill of wheeling that classic '55 down his home track, confirmed by his ever-present smile behind that oh-so-70s moustache.

When his interest in drag competition waned, he turned his attention to the street machine movement and, in particular, the Australian National Street Machine Association and its NSW division.

Stubbsy was a tireless campaigner for the street machine cause, and this is where I really came to know the man. At every opportunity, he would be representing ANSMA. Like a spruiker at a carnival, he would extol first the benefits of joining ANSMA and later the advantages of the street machine insurance scheme he pioneered.

The '55 was replaced by a Chevy Malibu four-door sedan. Not everyone's cup of tea as a project, but that was Graham – never one to run with the herd, always an individual.

Graham was a perfectionist. His skills as a carpenter and boat builder were to serve him well during the build of his Malibu, a car that scored over 400 trophies around the show circuit during its time.

"Stubbsy never rested on his laurels," says Summernats judge Owen Webb. "He was always improving the car. Every time I went to a show, he'd pull me aside to show me the latest mod, be it the perspex in the bonnet or a new custom piece he'd cast."

Graham used the same energy to fight for the sport itself. "He went in to bat for street machiners and spent a lot of time banging his head against the wall with rego authorities," says car builder Greg 'Ziggy' Sadler. "He got them to sit down and talk about modified cars, and that laid the foundation for what we have now."

STORY GEOFF PARADISE **PHOTOS** SM ARCHIVES

ABOVE: Graham's '65 Malibu (*SM*, Dec '81-Jan '82) brought new levels of detail to the show scene, while always being a proudly street-driven car. It won more than 400 awards between 1979 and 1993

OPPOSITE PAGE: Malibu Magic's current custodian is John McCoy-Lancaster, who, after 400 hours work, drove the car to Summernats 27 in 2014. "We don't call it a restoration, we call it a clean-up," says John. "We were committed to presenting it exactly as Graham last had it."
For John, the journey of bringing the car back into the limelight was deeply personal and gratifying. "I first saw Malibu Magic when I was 11. Graham and I struck up a conversation and he remembered me each year after that"

Racing at Castlereagh

Summernats 27

The Grot, '77

Johnny Wheeltubs

JOHN TAVERNA 1947–2013

DRAG RACER, PRO STREET KING AND SO MUCH MORE

HOW many street machines benefitted from the skills of the late John Taverna? Too many to count, but the list would include high-calibre SMOTY winners like Al 'Bundy' Lucas's HQ and two of Gary Myers's Mustangs.

John Taverna, the man they called 'Johnny Wheeltubs', was also a record-setting drag racer, a master race car constructor, a successful car importer at scale, an influential ANDRA heavyweight and a pioneering show judge.

The first phase of John's career was all about racing. While he had a day gig at the Ford factory, his debut down the quarter-mile was in 1968 in a '57 Chev, and he was instantly hooked. He took the Chev as far as it would go, and in 1975 partnered with Phil Facciolo on the first of three cars that would be dubbed The Grot. The first car was an FJ Holden that quickly nabbed them the B/Gas and C/Gas class records. Next was an HK Monaro powered by an injected 302 that drove them to victory at the Sportsnationals in 1977.

In 1979, John went solo for the final iteration of The Grot, an A/Gas Torana, which was followed by a B/Gas Commodore.

As demand for his expertise around chassiswork, ladder bars and wheel tubs grew, John began working out of his parents' garage on other people's cars, adding painting and panel beating to his list of skills. He'd also buy, fix and flip cars, all the while holding down a day job at Ford.

In 1982, he handed in his notice and launched John Taverna Chassis, which became an overwhelming success, producing quality work for luminaries like Peter Kapiris, Hans Van Dyk, the Sammut Brothers, Russell Simpson, Hugo Di Gianvincenzo, Ian McCurdy, Paul Rogers, Maurice Fabietti, Tony Harrington and many more.

John continued to race, most notably in a blown Holden JB Camira, before moving onto a green JD Camira in Pro Stock.

PREVIOUS PAGES (124-125): Lismore-based body man Dean Prodger purchased the ex-Taverna/Facciolo HK Monaro (the second incarnation of The Grot) on eBay in 2009 for $1600. Once he discovered its provenance, he committed himself to rebuilding it better-than-new, debuting the final results at MotorEx 2022

TOP LEFT: John's racing career started in earnest in 1975 when he teamed up with Phil Facciolo with their FJ Holden, The Grot

BOTTOM LEFT: The idea of building a cutting-edge race car out of a front-wheel-drive Camira was shocking in the early 80s, but JT did it with great success

John's '68 Mustang

Silver Bullet build

XB in the USA

ABOVE: Taverna astride an in-the-build Silver Bullet in 2003. "JT's impact on my life is hard to put into words," says Gary Myers. "He was my mate and mentor; he inspired and supported me in every major build"

John's most famous street car was his '67 big-block Camaro (*SM*, Apr-May '91). Built in four months, he drove it to Summernats 4, blew minds and won Top Super Street

'67 big-block Camaro

468ci big-block

He also got involved on the admin side, acting as ANDRA Victorian divisional director and deputy national director, helping steer the sport during a tumultuous period. It was a big task, so much so that he stepped back from racing in 1990. While he continued to build drag cars and serve that community, John's street machine phase had begun, and with the rise of the pro street movement, the timing could not have been better.

His first foray into building a streeter for himself was a pink 308-powered LJ Torana. Built as a street-legal showcase, the job was covered extensively in *Street & Custom* mag. That was just a warm-up. His '67 Camaro (*SM*, Apr-May '91) was a stunning four-month build that he drove from Melbourne to Canberra for its Summernats debut, where it won Top Super Street.

Killer customer cars followed, including John Batten's outrageous pro street Willys (*SM*, Sep '92).

As he'd done with drag racing, John also gave back to the sport of street machining at the highest levels, first conducting packed-out seminars on car crafting at Summernats, before joining the judging team for the best part of a decade. He later acted as the Grand Marshal for Perth's Motorvation event.

Always looking for new opportunities, John ramped up the import side of his business, making multiple trips to the US every year to bring back container-loads of parts and whole cars. He ultimately specialised in Mustangs, producing turn-key dreamboats for many happy customers.

John passed away in August 2013, but John Taverna Chassis continues to this day, with long-time employee Adrian Sankovic running things.

John was posthumously awarded Rare Spares Legend status in 2014 and was inducted into the ANDRA Hall of Fame in 2015. Fittingly, the Summernats Master Craftsman Award was renamed the John Taverna Memorial Award in his honour and is a much-prized commendation for those at the pinnacle of their craft.

TOP RIGHT: Taverna's workshop turned out many great race cars of the 1980s and 90s; probably the best-known is Peter Kapiris's AA/Gas Chevy Beretta

RIGHT: See that HQ Monaro hanging above JT's head? That's Al 'Bundy' Lucas's SMOTY winner. Queenslander Al met JT at a Melbourne car show and within weeks had left his perfectly awesome HQ at JTC for a full-chassis job. Bundy even accompanied JT on a US trip to work and buy parts for the build

STORY SIMON TELFORD **PHOTOS** *SM* ARCHIVES

TOP: The FJ won Street Machine of the Year in '94 and scooped Top Mild Custom, Top Bodywork and Judges' Choice at Summernats in 1995

LEFT & ABOVE: Colin sold the FJ to good mate Kevin Brown, who looks after it like a newborn. He brought it back to Canberra for Summernats in 2014, where it blew the minds of a whole new generation

COLIN TOWNSEND

SOME folks see so far ahead, the rest of the world never catches up. Adelaide's Colin Townsend is that kind of visionary. This was evident from the very first car of his that we featured – a subtle powder-blue FJ Holden (*SM*, Apr-May '83), sitting down hard over fat Pirellis on steel wheels.

With a hot 186 and a single-rail 'box, the humpy was tidy, but on a quick scan it didn't look anything cutting-edge. Anyone who delved a little deeper would discover that while the raw materials were standard 80s fare, the application of them was not. The whole car was designed to give the best possible compromise between ride and handling on the road and track. As a result, the FJ batted far above its weight and was capable of dispatching Bolwell Nagaris around Mallala.

But the blue FJ – along with a similar FX powered by a turbo red that ran as quick as 13.3 seconds in the 70s – was just a trial run for the machine that brought all of Colin's philosophies about car building to life – his epic SMOTY-winning FJ.

His ambitions were lofty: "I wanted to build the ultimate street-legal performance car. I wanted it to be unbreakable, have plenty of visual appeal and handle like a circuit car, yet be refined enough for road use."

The result was a masterpiece, with massive rubber covered in all-steel pumped guards, a 500hp 308 recessed deep into the firewall for optimum weight distribution, and much more. It was fully legal in South Australia, which was no mean feat in those days. I got the chance to drive the car in 2004, and it remains the most well-sorted highly modified car I've ever had the privilege to test.

Like Mark Sanders's LH Torana and Craig Parker's XY, Colin's FJ foreshadowed the pro touring scene that has been big in the States for years but never really caught on in any great fashion Down Under.

Colin pivoted to a Mopar in the late 90s, with a turbo, LPG-fed Hemi-six making over 500hp in a VG Valiant (*SM*, Jan-Feb '99) that he built for his missus, Violet. Another car that was way ahead of its time.

STORY SIMON TELFORD **PHOTOS** *SM* ARCHIVES

130

Violet's VG Valiant

308·053

SOUTH AUST.

SMOTY at speed

131

"The ute was my first car ever featured in a magazine — *Custom Vans & Trucks*," Owen says. "It was also David Fetherston's last-ever Aussie shoot for *Street Machine*" (Jan-Feb '86)

OWEN WEBB

OWEN Webb is the man with his finger on the pulse of the show-car scene. For almost 30 years, he has been a judge at *Street Machine* Summernats and other events, and he continues to keep tabs on what's being built, guides and encourages the builders, and curates the iconic unveilings of new elite rides at both the 'Nats and Meguiar's MotorEx. He's also taught generations of tradespeople about the fine art of custom paint.

Owen grew up on a dairy farm in the Southern Highlands region of New South Wales. "The farm gave me a love of tools and fixing things, but the day I finished my school certificate, I started an apprenticeship as a spray painter and panel beater at the Bowral Ford dealership," he says.

That dealership is where Owen acquired what was to become his first serious street machine, an XW Falcon ute named Bruiser (*SM*, Jan-Feb '86). "I'd owned a few EJ Holdens with lace paint and all that good stuff, but it was the ute that really got me hooked on the whole car scene," he says. "The XW was a six-cylinder trade-in that a local earthmoving guy had brought in. It was pretty knocked around. I gave it a cheap paintjob and drove it for four years before taking it off the road for a proper rebuild with good paint and a 351 Cleveland swap."

Other mods included velour trim (both in the cabin and the tray!), flared rear guards in steel, XW GT chin spoiler, a Blue Oval logo etched into the rear window, and the ubiquitous letterbox scoop. "I took it to a lot of shows – Roselands, Yennora, Orange, Wollongong, Albury Street Rod show," recalls Owen. "I took it to the fourth Street Machine Nationals in Narrandera, Easter 1980; that was a huge show. I did the first Summernats in that car, went in all the driving events, even the burnouts held on the main drag."

Owen's next car, an XY sedan dubbed Wild Thing (*SM*, Apr-May '88) really put him on the map. "What I wanted was a proper pro streeter; a car that was still recognisable as an XY but built like a race car everywhere else," he said at the time.

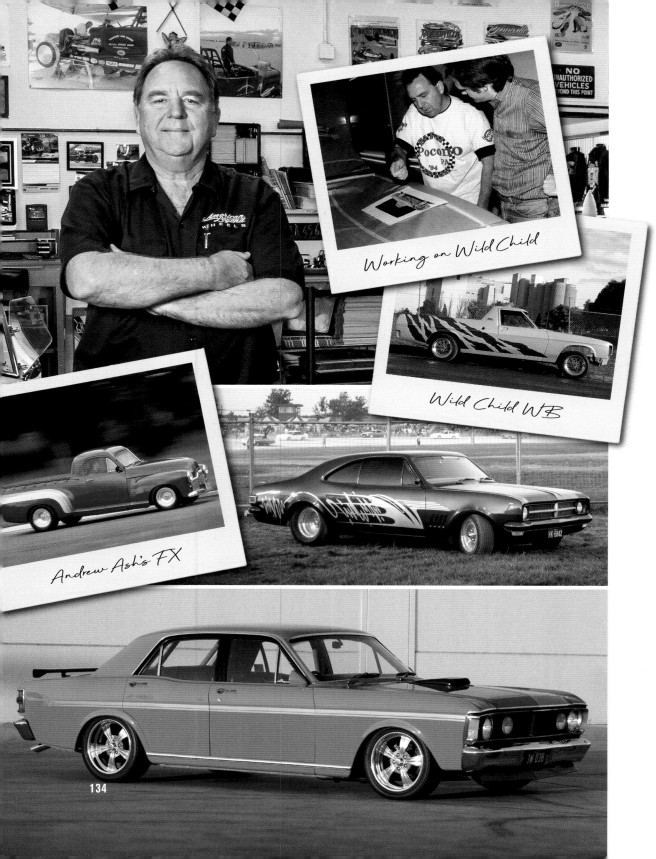

LEFT: Owen took care of the graphics on *Street Machine*'s Wild Child WB project car

MIDDLE RIGHT: Owen was the panel and paint man on Brian Willis's HK Monaro, which won the Grand Champion sword at Summernats in 1995 and then earned spots in the Top 10 for the next seven events!

MIDDLE LEFT: Paint guru Andrew Ash got his start as Owen's apprentice, during which time Owen applied the paint and graphics to the young Andrew's FX Holden ute

BOTTOM LEFT: Owen's current stable of cars includes this sweet XY GS (*SM*, Aug '05), which features a Ben Gatt-built 351

Working on Wild Child

Wild Child WB

Andrew Ash's FX

The interior featured lots of painted sheet metal, and its smoothed engine bay set the yardstick for all future Ford guys. Owen took the graphic-enhanced pro streeter to the first *Street Machine* Summernats, where it took out Top Undercarriage and Top Driveline, plus a spot in the Top10.

By this time, Owen had long finished his apprenticeship and was running his own restoration shop, Pro Finish, in Moss Vale. A bloke named Chic Henry soon came calling and invited him to join the Summernats judging team. Owen was impressed with Chic's vision to raise the standard of judging and came aboard for Summernats 3.

"Chic believed that if Summernats didn't drive innovation and excellence, people would simply keep building the same cars for the next 20 years," he says. "I agree, and have really encouraged builders to get innovative to give everyone else something to step up to."

After Pro Finish, Owen went to work for Dulux and later House of Kolor and others, developing product, techniques and talent.

He also devised specialist paint application training programs and then taught them at TAFEs and other organisations around Australia, including in remote areas.

All the while, he's stayed hands-on. The panel and paint on Brian Willis's iconic HK Monaro was Owen's doing, as were both versions of Howard Astill's XA coupe. He also helped out doing the flames and pinstripes on Gary Myers's Silver Bullet Mustang.

He's built a few cars for himself, including a sweet XY GS Falcon (*SM*, Aug '06) and a '69 Camaro. He was even on the team that built the State Coach Britannia for the British royal family in 2005.

And, while his cars have always won trophies, so has Owen himself, including being inducted into the Rare Spares Hall of Fame in 2011, and receiving the Medal of the Order of Australia (OAM) in 2015.

STORY SIMON TELFORD **PHOTOS** *SM* ARCHIVES

Owen and Jack Trepanier

Summernats 1

Owen, Chic and Andy Lopez

The Wild Thing XY was bought as an unfinished project, complete with a full chassis and 22in tubs courtesy of a young Murray Anderson. Its wild graphics and lurid rear end were plastered across the cover of *Street Machine*'s March '88 issue as part of the huge Summernats 1 coverage, but readers had to wait until the April-May edition for a full feature

135

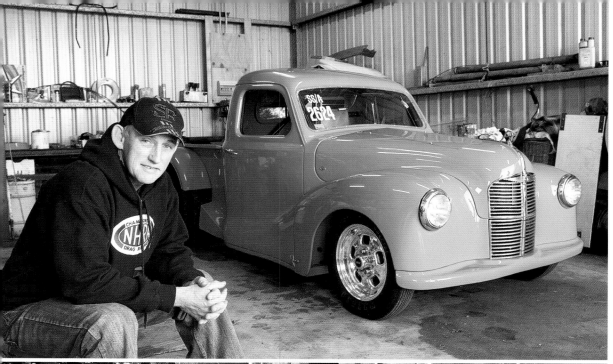

TOP: After many years away from the strip, Rex returned to drag racing for the adrenaline rush. Following a brief stint racing a big-block Chev-powered One Tonner, he purchased this ex-Mal Gower Supercharged Outlaws Austin A40 ute. In true Rex form, the ute scored a show-quality ground-up rebuild and was soon running into the nines

ABOVE: The lidless Karmann Ghia was Rex's follow-up to the FJ build and blew minds with its ground-scraping stance, killer graphics and radical design

REX WEBSTER

ALTHOUGH it never scored the front cover of *Street Machine* (our giveaway A9X trumped it in *SM*, Dec '86), nothing could stop Rex Webster's FJ Holden becoming the most influential car of its time.

Created in partnership with Rex's brother Tony, the FJ was originally their drag car, converted to a two-door and fitted with a stove-hot red.

After a five-year build that saw the brothers close their panel shop to concentrate obsessively on the FJ, the machine they debuted at the 1986 Rickshaws show in Newcastle changed the game forever.

Why? For starters, the FJ's undercarriage featured hand-beaten surfaces that were better than many show car exteriors. Every cast part on the car was ground down, smoothed off and painted to perfection. Dozens of billet aluminium parts were hand made, and it had a tubular front end – likely the first in Oz. And not forgetting the innovative touch-control panel for all the major functions of the car, which gave the FJ its name, High Tech. It was next-level stuff, and the young guns of the day paid attention.

"I remember one bloke in particular, Ron Barclay, he really got into the detail of it," says Rex. "Without a word of a lie, he spent three days looking at my car at the Melbourne Hot Rod Show. I don't think he left my stand."

The FJ won Top Judged at the very first Summernats in January 1988 before being shipped to the US, where it took out a raft of awards – including Top Custom Car at the invite-only Fresno Autorama in '89 – and being road-tripped between events to boot.

After a year in the US showing the car and working for Fat Jack Enterprises, Rex brought the FJ home, put it away and focused on his innovative Karmann Ghia.

Disillusioned by the economics of building cars for a living, Rex dropped out of the scene and pivoted to building horse floats. After two decades, he came full circle and got back into drag racing.

The FJ was eventually sold and has returned to the show scene in a couple of guises since. But its original form, in the hands of Rex, will always be the standard by which others are measured.

STORY SIMON MAJOR **PHOTOS** PETER BATEMAN & *SM* ARCHIVES

Rex's FJ blew the doors off Aussie street machining, with amazing attention to detail that conquered not just the Australian show scene but the US as well. The car scooped the pool when it toured the States, winning trophies at events including the Street Machine Olympics, the Oakland Roadster Show and Fresno Autorama

Summernats 1

FJ in '86

Hunchback build

STEPHEN WILSON

DURING the 1970s and early 80s, creativity was king in the Australian hot car scene. Raw materials were cheap and the panel van craze pushed builders into an arms race of insane paint, panel and trim jobs. Stephen and Rowan Wilson were two of the most creative guys on the scene in NSW, their work acting as a sort of connective tissue between the vanning and street machine movements.

As well as being a major influence on the next generation of builders – Ziggy Sadler for one – the brothers were also pivotal players in the early days of the NSW Street Machine Association at a time when the sport was just starting to organise itself.

Stephen cut his teeth on a MkII Ford Zephyr in the early 70s, customising it with rollpans, sidepipes, a peaked grille and shaved door handles. It was a classic Aussie custom, such as had been madly popular throughout the suburbs in the 60s. His next builds, however, looked to the future.

His audacious HT ute, dubbed Bewitched, sported a tube grille, XC Fairmont headlights and XW Falcon tail-lights, custom paint, sail panels and a rear wing, powered by a tunnel-rammed 308.

Steve's builds were ever-evolving, and he transformed the ute into the Devil's Delivery by sheeting in the sides from the roof back to the wing and adding a TC Cortina wagon tailgate.

He soon turned his passion into a business, running Auto Art Custom Paint & Body Shop in Katoomba, NSW.

Next came one of the most radical builds ever seen in Australia, an HT van-meets-HK Monaro dubbed Hunchback. Steve took his daily-driver HT, picked up a damaged HK Monaro shell from the local tip and got busy. He cut the turret and rear quarters off the van and matched it to the Monaro roof and boot profile, before adding an array of other custom features.

Hunchback debuted at the 1980 Street Machine Nationals and spent the next five years on the show circuit – while constantly evolving – before being sold and lost to time.

STORY SIMON MAJOR **PHOTOS** BRYCE FORREST & *SM* ARCHIVES

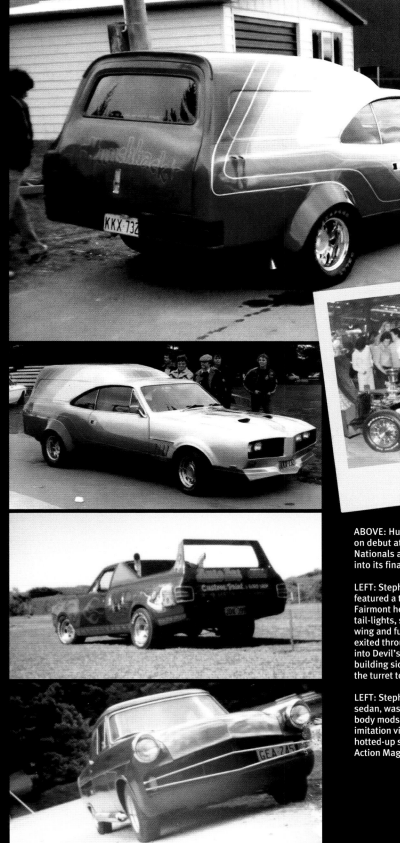

Hunchback

ABOVE: Hunchback wowed the crowds on debut at the 1980 Street Machine Nationals and evolved over five years into its final form pictured here

LEFT: Stephen's Bewitched HT ute featured a tube grille and rollpans, XC Fairmont headlights and XW Falcon tail-lights, sail panels for the sides, a rear wing and functioning truck stacks that exited through the tray. It later morphed into Devil's Delivery, with Stephen building sides and a roof panel to join the turret to the rear wing

LEFT: Stephen's first car, a MkII Zephyr sedan, was customised with period body mods, custom lace paintwork and imitation vinyl roof. The Zephyr ran a hotted-up six-cylinder and rolled on 13in Action Mags wheels

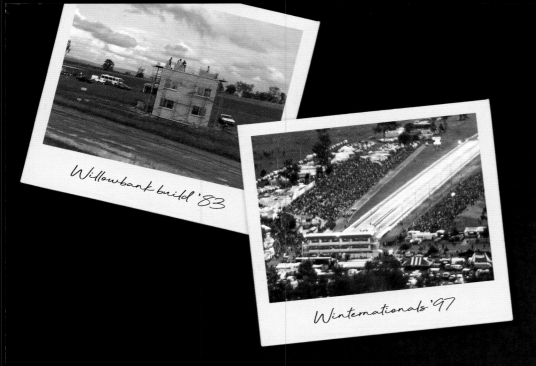

Willowbank build '83

Winternationals '97

Glen Burns's Escort

ABOVE: When Glen Burns's Escort
hit the Surfers Christmas Tree at the
1981 Nationals, the meeting had to be
halted as there were no spare bulbs!
This was the final straw for Stomper
and Syrmis, who decided on the spot
to build their own track

JOHN WINTERBURN 1947-2020
& DENNIS SYRMIS 1942-2013

OUR sport owes much to those who have fought over the years to provide places where we can safely play away from the long arm of the law. There are too many of these heroes to pay tribute to them all, though we should give a shout-out to the late Gary Miocevich, who was responsible for the design, development and construction of the Perth Motorplex, which opened in 2000.

Queenslanders John 'Stomper' Winterburn and Dennis Syrmis did the same for Queensland in the early 80s, when it was apparent that the Surfers Paradise track would not survive the property boom on the Gold Coast.

"In 1981, we set up a not-for-profit, Willowbank Raceway Inc., and I became the president," recalled Stomper. "We were offered land to lease and set about building a drag strip."

Starting with a bare block of land and no money, a core group of volunteers spent four years working every weekend when there was no race meeting at Surfers. "There was no government assistance, just hard work and negotiations," Stomper said. "We decided to build all of the track ourselves, except the strip surface."

When it came to securing the $250,000 needed to bitumen the track, Stomper was pivotal in lobbying for funds and is revered as one of the 'Willowbank Seven' from the management committee who signed mortgage documents on their own houses guaranteeing the loan.

The project took five years but had positive implications for the sport nationwide. The fact that Willowbank was up and running when Surfers was suddenly shut down in 1987 meant that Queensland did not suffer the dire consequences of having a capital city without the services of a track, as happened in Sydney (twice), Melbourne, Adelaide and Canberra. Simply put, during parts of the 80s, 90s and 2000s, Australian drag racing survived because Willowbank held the sport together as the only continuously operating capital-city track on the east coast.

Dennis was manager of Willowbank until 2002 and passed in 2013 at the age of 71. Stomper passed in 2020 at 72, having served drag racing for 53 years.

STORY LEX SWAYN **PHOTOS** PETER BATEMAN & *SM* ARCHIVES

ABOVE & RIGHT: Prior to running Willowbank, Dennis Syrmis was an influential director of ANDRA. He introduced dial-your-own racing, which grew the sport exponentially by opening up the drag strip to a wider range of competitors

Dennis Syrmis

BELOW: Dennis started drag racing on the streets of Brisbane at age 18 in 1960, but even then he was an organiser, timing the runs with a stopwatch and recording them for posterity. When drag racing went legit, first at Lowood and then Surfers Paradise, Dennis was right amongst it in his Time Machine FJ Holden. Later on he ran Corolla and Escort gassers

John 'Stomper' Winterburn

ABOVE (L-R): Andrew Lynch,
Rebecca Lynch (née Zelukovic),
Jeromie Zelukovic, John
Zelukovic (seated), Ron
Zelukovic, Ben Zelukovic

LEFT: Ben Zelukovic's Escort
has featured in magazines and
run 12.0 at the drags, but still
sees its share of circle work.
He's currently working on
a slammed, V8-powered Toyota
Lite Stout

Ben's Escort

BELOW: The metal-working
skills of Ron and Tom Zelukovic
were on full display on Darryl
McBeth's radical two-door
Magna (*SM*, Oct '04)

JOHN & RON ZELUKOVIC

LIKE many brothers, Ron and John Zelukovic are the same but different. John is the more driven and outwardly successful, while Ron has long followed his own muse. Between them and their older brother Tom, who passed away in 2012, the Orange, NSW-based siblings have built hundreds of cars, many of them iconic.

From a very early age, the Zelukovic boys were expected to give their old man Rista a hand in his canvas shed. "I can recall my father asking me to pass him a 9/16th spanner when I was about five," Ron says. "I couldn't even count to 10. We didn't know any different."

By the tender age of 12, John had souped up a Morris Eight roadster. Then came a succession of customised FJ Holdens. He fitted a 292 Y-block Ford V8 to one of them way back in 1965, before he had a licence.

Ron started at a similar age. "I was 13 or 14 when I built an engine by myself," he recalls. "Dad said if I bought him a box of tallnecks he'd show me how to do it, but he just took the bottles inside the house and left me to it. My first registered car was an EH I built when I was 16. It had Valiant Charger grilles, massive flares, 10-inch racing tyres on the back and was tubbed to the rails."

As adults, the brothers continued to build cars for themselves and others. Their collaborations include Darryl McBeth's Magna, Mario Colalillo's King Cad, and the radical pro street 1960 Studebaker owned by John's wife Rhonda that sent the Aussie show car scene into spasms at Summernats 10.

John built a successful smash repair and custom car building business that employed as many as 40 people, sufficient to fund excursions into both Wild Bunch and Funny Car racing.

Ron has lost count of the number of hot rods he's had a hand in but is most proud of a coupe he built out of a roadster in the 80s. "It was the first smoothed '34 three-window in Australia," he says.

"Ron started a lot of trends with that car," John adds.

The fruit has not fallen far from the tree. Both Ron's daughter Nardia and John's son Ben had upbringings not dissimilar to their dads', at least as far as cars are concerned. These days Ben is a respected car builder in his own right and runs the family business with his sister Rebecca, whose husband Andrew Lynch is also a skilled car crafter.

John and Ron give full credit to their dad Rista for the family's skills. "The knowledge our father had was incredible," John says. "He had some funny philosophies but he taught us there's nothing we can't do."

STORY GEOFF SEDDON **PHOTOS** PETER BATEMAN & *SM* ARCHIVES